APOSTOL

Critical Tools to I

Ordained Mentor

THERESA HARVARD JOHNSON

Theresa Harvard Johnson
950 Eagles Landing Parkway, Ste. 302
Stockbridge, GA 30281

Printed in the United States of America.
2017 First Edition
ISBN-13: 978-1976319938
ISBN-10: 1976319935

DEDICATION

To Dr. Kluane Spake, mother of my heart,
because you were delighted to share
God's good news and your own life
with His people.

ACKNOWLEDGEMENTS

I wish to thank Apostle Dr. Kluane Spake, the intimate apostolic mentor God sent me as I cried out to him in my prayers. Truly you have begotten me as a daughter in the Gospel. Thank you for being as excited about this project as I was when the Lord showed it to me in a dream. I couldn't have written it without your most excellent example, wisdom, insight, direction and significant input. This is "our" book.

I thank my former Pastor Eddie Mason and Minister Beverly Gammalo. You demonstrated the love of God in my life at a level I have not seen in a congregational setting. My restoration from tremendous childhood and church hurt began with you. Thank you for your time, investment, full acceptance, encouragement and love through Christ. You set foundations in my life concerning *pure* ministry and *pure* mentorship.

I thank Belinda Beach, Bernard Boulton, Terrance L. Frederick and Andrea Renfroe for their candid testimonies concerning their mentoring experiences. You represent so many people who have walked through some hard places and learned invaluable lessons. I also want to thank Andrea Renfroe for reading the finished manuscript in advance to advise me on its flow, comprehension and readability for audiences of all levels of the faith. I also want to thank Christine Lombard for extensive review and editing.

I thank my husband Leonard Johnson Jr., who stands as my protector, always wanting to make sure that no one wounds my heart in the name of the Gospel. Thank you for walking with me into victory in Christ.

TABLE OF CONTENTS

INTRODUCTION

Not everyone wants a mentor or believes they need one. I understand that. It is okay because our lives, callings, and goals are as different as we are as individuals.

Many of us have had mentors. We've needed a tutor in a school subject, have had to learn a sport or were discipled by someone in the faith – whether it was a pastor, neighbor, parent or Sunday school teacher.

Perhaps how we choose to define the term mentor is our greatest challenge because it means different things to different people.

What we need to know when reading this book, *"Apostolic Mentoring: Critical Tools to Help Artisans Identify Their God Ordained Mentor,"* is that mentoring can be defined as loosely or as intimately as one desires.

The definition we will use is this: A mentor is an experienced, confidential and trusted advisor, counselor or guide who helps someone navigate a specific area in their life, career, ministry or other area under a high level of knowledge and expertise in the hope of achieving success for the mentee. While we will discuss varying kinds of mentorship, this book is focused primarily on those who are seeking and in need of **INTIMATE,** apostolic, one-on-one *spiritual* mentoring relationships.

I am convinced there is a special anointing upon believers in the creative community in the church today. This book is written in hopes of helping creatives (worshippers, scribes and artisans) connect with the right mentor and avoid the tremendous pitfalls associated with mentorship.

I have had an extremely difficult time in ministry. My journey was exacerbated in my specific community as an artisan due to the lack of value, respect and honor in ministry environments concerning my calling to scribal ministry or the arts. The calling into apostolic ministry placed me in an entirely new category of peculiar.

Out of safety, protection and a desire for prophetic artistic community, some artisans are creating their own worship and teaching hubs. God is raising up mentors for them and expanding the comprehension of their unique calling.

This underground movement is rising from the ashes and redefining what "church" looks like. Their thrust for worship and a longing for the creative demonstration of the Kingdom through the arts is so intense that it is challenging congregations globally to take notice of their approach.

Apostolic and prophetic leaders who are creatives or who have a creative ear have been relentlessly shouting this truth across our congregations for years. I stand as one of those apostolic voices and forerunners in this movement in my specific metron – the office of the prophetic scribe. There is a push in the 21st century toward authentic and organic creative worship. I am completely overwhelmed by those I am encountering who are hearing the same message; and walking out what they hear with such fierceness. In our community, we are upon a significant prophetic, creative wave unlike anything seen in the history of the congregation.

As the face of the local congregation continues to change and more people exit the traditional structure of the local church, worship arts communities seem to be emerging as full ministries, community groups, worship teams and other organizational forms independent of the local congregation.

Whether a particular group or denomination considers this a healthy formation or not, it doesn't change the fact that it is happening. Through this, I firmly believe Father is crying out for drastic change in our congregational communities. Like me, so many people need a different kind of ministry environment. I was desperate to engage in my creative calling and see where it would take me. The only way to do this was to step away from traditional structures and forge a new path fully directed by Holy Spirit. I loved the local congregation (and still do), but I was unable to soar within the confines of its system all those years ago. Graduation was at hand. Unfortunately, I had no idea where a passionate worshipper, scribe and artisan like me could go to engage.

Telling someone I was called to restore the ministry of the prophetic scribe within the Kingdom met hordes of laughter, disbelief and accusations of arrogance. It was an "impossible thing" for people in my environment to see or even want to see the potential in "the office of the scribe" beyond the gift of prophetic writing. Yet there I was with this unquenchable, burning, insane desire to see it come forth. I am so thankful to God for being fearless in the pursuit of my calling.

I learned early on that I was a part of a new generation of worshippers whom the Lord was raising up to redefine and lead many aspects of the 21st century congregation. This place of definition, however, was never one of abandoning God's plan for the local congregation and going freestyle Theresa's way. I understood that I needed structure, order, leadership and protocol. I understood the need for deep rooted equipping in biblical foundations.

I also knew that sound biblical teaching and seasoned leadership was at the core of whatever direction the Lord placed before me in prayer, discipleship, leadership development, healing in community, accountability and all those other elements required to build God's army.

What I didn't need was all the religiosity, manipulation, control and the limited view of the arts that often came with mainstream ministry structures regardless of denomination.

I also didn't need anything that stifled my God given creativity, growth and progress. I was sick and tired of seeing worship and the arts regulated to special events, weddings, funerals and holiday focused, event based ministry. I wanted to see our creative gifts as a main vein in ministry, able to sustain the community with the same power as a preaching or prayer ministry.

Either **1 Corinthians 12** was accurate or it was not. Who are we to decide what has the greatest or least impact in the hearts of men? Only the Lord gets to decide that with the gifts and callings placed in our hands. Shouldn't we all have an opportunity to explore the depth of what is in us? Moses had a staff. David had a harp, music sheets and a slingshot. Miriam had dance. But they all brought forth the message of reconciliation.

I was of the mind that the Gospel could be preached in a number of creative ways and environments, and be just as effective as a sermon or a Bible study within the right structure and with the appropriate balance.

In my time in ministry, I've found this to be true not only from an evangelistic perspective but in fortifying biblical principles and concepts through prophetic demonstration while preaching and teaching. And guess what? I've met growing communities of us from all over the world who share a similar vision that is completely led of Holy Spirit.

It blesses me tremendously to see an increasing number of mainstream congregations operating this way.

My heart burns for immersion – the fullness of reconciliation in me and in the Body. I long to see the people of God embrace the beauty of Christ in and around them in all its facets. I can still remember the night of December 31, 2000 when the Spirit said to me, "I will use your creative writing gift to be a voice for Christ and to bring forth a harvest." I had no idea of what this meant at the time, but I do today. Truly, God has done that over the years and I anticipate Him doing so much more. I am wise enough to know, however, that my calling in this area would have dried up and died had I stayed in the structure of the traditional Protestant congregation that was before me.

I wanted Christ and His precious community, but I didn't want the confines of the institution that limited my creative worship capacity. I needed structure and strong teaching, but I also needed the freedom to soar and obtain an aerial view of my calling and purpose. I recognized that I needed mentorship to get to the point of soaring, and I was desperate for it.

In different seasons of my life I've been like Moses, Abraham, Isaac and Jacob, walking alone, in agony for help that only God could provide. I've been like Onesimus, needing a mentor to usher me into healing and into a place of profitability when I was no more than a thief. I've been like Joshua, Elisha and Samuel, needing a mentor to teach me intimately and/or journey with me up close or from afar.

I've been like Ruth to Naomi and Samuel to a *corrupt* Eli, standing in mentoring situations due to desperation or a result of no plan of my own, and had to claw my way out and into a healthy place. I've been like Luke, Timothy, Titus and Tertius to Paul, maturing in my gifting and calling while co-laboring under a profound example of faithfulness to God.

I stood in some ways like Paul – recognizing that I needed rescue, wisdom, connection, friendship, counsel, guidance and the experience of Barnabas at the epoch of my ministry maturation and calling. For me, God sent Dr. K.

While not everyone needs a mentor, some people have been ordained to be mentored! This isn't giving man power or control over us. This is not about forsaking God's strength in our lives and relying on men.

Let's put away that thinking right now! Mentorship is a demonstration of Sonship – in heaven and in the earth. It is a cry to the son to listen to the instructions of the Father. It is the hope of the older women to teach the younger. It is an ancient pattern of a teacher-student that can be seen throughout the scriptures and even our society today. It is recognizing a need for assistance and support in fortifying our calling, purpose and destiny. And as we can see from both biblical covenants, God has ordained all kinds of mentoring relationships, regardless of whether or not we identify with every one of them. By using myself in these examples, I am simply expressing how we might see and comprehend mentorship as discussed in this book.

Finally, remember that the life or even the lifestyle of an artisan isn't understood by everyone. While people appreciate creativity and art – prophetic or nonprophetic, few have compassion for the plight of the artisan. Likewise, few long to see creative communities emerge as a leading force or a local entity organized like a congregation. I have experienced extreme hostility in this area with ministers accustomed to church-setup given us by what is theologically understood as the church establishment of the early church father. As a result, it is quite difficult to lead or guide someone in an area that a person may not honor, respect or see at the magnitude needed to lead others. I recognize this as a mentor and as a mentee.

I've had leaders who couldn't "behold" me – see what was presently in me or what was to come. Rather they wanted to make me in their image. I've also had to repent for doing this to others along my journey! I am so thankful I know better now!

I was told once that the ministry entrusted to me was no more than an evangelistic outreach that should be a part of a full congregation. I have been encouraged countless times by ministers to launch a traditional church structure. I cannot begin to tell you how deeply I struggled with this concept. I knew the prophetic words and insight they offered had validity, but how that model was to look was still beyond my grasp of understanding.

Efforts to explain what I saw always fell on deaf ears as assumptions were made that I was talking about dismantling the "local church" pattern pioneered by Paul. Never once did any of those specific leaders take the time to hear my heart! How many more people are there in this same situation?

Your circumstances are probably different, but the dilemma is the same: **"Where can you find the right kind of help?"**

What I was doing at the time had not been done before in my sphere of influence. Countless people, including influential ministers from around the globe, have told me that the ministry entrusted to me was a first in the earth. When I first began, we were pushing forth in healing nights, weekly prayer meetings, bible studies, and evangelistic services through poetry, spoken word and the arts as if it were a revival service. There was leadership, discipleship, evangelism and clearly, I was an active and present pastor to the people I was leading.

What if I had believed what those leaders said? What if I had relegated the vision entrusted to me to fundraisers, Easter programs and Christmas plays? What if I had allowed the institution of the church in the Bible belt to dictate my identity as a scribe and artisan? What if my understanding of MYSELF was limited to someone else's ceiling-to-floor mentality? Listen, you and I would not be meeting in this moment had I conformed and blended into those ideals; though I am sure the intent was mostly good by those who wanted to help.

That kind of help just wasn't for me!

Prayerfully, I'm speaking to others in similar situations who need help navigating into their next natural and spiritual place. Maybe you have a longing or a cry in your heart for apostolic mentorship right now... and God placed it there. Perhaps you have this spiritual thirst for something bigger than you and need to connect with that "one thing" you can't put your finger on to get you there. Maybe you simply need an uncommon, apostolic thrust to catapult you into a critical crossover point in your journey – whether temporal or long-term. You might need an apostolic mentor who is a divine, seasoned strategist with the natural and heavenly access to help you cross over and into the fullness of your purpose and destiny! It is okay if you do.

In this book, I am sharing the wisdom and insight I have gained not only as a mentee, but also as an active prophetic artisan who mentors other apostles, prophets, pastors, evangelists and teachers called to scribal ministry and the worship arts. It is my hope that creatives can identify and connect with apostolic mentors who have a heart for them, their calling and the creative community after reading it while also understanding how to properly respond to that mentor.

Finally, I hope to present a clear picture of what healthy mentorship might look like while making immature, abusive, unhealthy relationships *clear and easy* to identify. I am desperate to expose the hireling, the pimp and the prostitute that chases after the worshipper, scribe and the artisan.

I'm drawing as much from my own mistakes and successes as a mentor as I am from my experiences as a mentee – this includes the good, the bad and the ugly. I haven't been a perfect mentor or mentee in my lifetime, but I hope that I have learned from my mistakes. I promise you truth in the Lord as I see it, and authenticity in my approach. My intent is not to exhaust this topic, but to provide some basic information that you can build upon. I pray that this book is a resource that you will glean from; and use as a teaching tool to impart, build and strengthen mentoring relationships within your own life and perhaps, your rising or existing community. May you long for true covenantal connection in Christ in your mentoring relationships and honor Christ in all your efforts.

Embracing IMMERSION,

Theresa Harvard Johnson

Remember those leaders who led you,
who spoke the word of God to you;
and considering the result of their conduct,
imitate their faith.
~Hebrews 13:7

NAVIGATION IS EVERYTHING

"How can I help you?"

These five words caused a sudden quiet to sweep through our corner of Starbucks.

I was enjoying a hot cup of black tea with cream and honey with Dr. Kluane Spake, an apostle I had only met in person a few weeks prior in hopes of gaining a spiritual mentor to help me navigate my apostolic calling. It was winter, and there she was sipping a cold Frappuccino caught in a gaze that seemed to bore a hole right through me.

At that time, I was still a little intimidated by apostolic leaders. This step was huge for me.

Honestly, I wasn't prepared to respond to such a bold question. I was conditioned to leaders selling me on a program, a mentoring class or another network gathering which is extremely popular within apostolic-prophetic communities. I was completely caught off guard by her question. She wanted to know *how she* could help *me*. I could feel my emotions rising as water formed around the brim of my eyes threatening to expose how touched I was by this exchange.

About three months prior, I was sitting before my computer crying out to the Lord for help in my apostolic journey. I couldn't find the kind of connection at the level I needed around me. Either those who extended help were too busy or they wanted to shuffle me into premade programs, classes, books, groups or elaborate networks that were not profitable for me and labeled with wild expectations.

At the end of the day, those options did not meet the unique challenges I faced as a leader called to national and international scribal ministry, worship and the arts.

I lost count of how many of these groups I was pulled into looking for help. One group, a large network based out of a major city on the east coast, would hold packed out meetings here in the Atlanta area bi-monthly. They would bring in major speakers, well-known prophets and provide resources I thought I needed. I enjoyed the teachings, but disliked the prophecy times and the setup for ministry giving. Every opportunity for prophecy and healing was ladled in a *ridiculous* amount of financial expectation. I am not exaggerating here.

As an artist and worshipper, I needed an apostolic-prophetic, creative environment and community that not only provided strong teaching, but also accountability and help! I needed to take home more than just revelation. I needed practical strategy and guidance to help me navigate this season of my life in the natural and in the Spirit. I couldn't get that from these types of meetings or leaders. I knew the Lord had more for me.

I was in agony concerning how to process all the things that were happening in my life, and how to shift with the waves as they came. My travel schedule had intensified nationally and internationally. I was learning to balance my home life during these changes, complete my Masters of Divinity degree and gain footing within my existing ministry activities. It was as if the prophesies released over my life in the last decade decided to crash land between 2013 and 2014, and instead of being overjoyed, I was overwhelmed and quite honestly, afraid. What can be done when that happens except try to stay above water? No one explained how to prepare for something like this and I surely didn't expect it.

The apostolic leaders whom I thought would help never had time for me when I needed it most. There was little opportunity to ask questions, to get help or to build relationship outside of these networks. In addition, the groups consisted of traditional apostles and pastors whose ministry models and needs were completely unrelated to mine. I was still an outsider in some of these settings because of the focus of what was in my hand. As a result, there was always this underlining desire to "rehabilitate" my thinking.

All I knew to do was to continue to trust God. If I were to align with someone full-force they would need a heart for me. They would take the time to at least listen to the leading of the Lord I felt inside my heart and build help for me around it. While I was frustrated, I never became angry or bitter. I realize leaders are often in demand, walking out their own vision, attending to their existing mentees, and cannot mentor everyone they meet intimately. So, if they could not see me or my need, then more than likely they were not the **INTIMATE** mentor for me.

I knew in my heart it was God's will that I have an **INTIMATE** mentor, and that the mentor be apostolic. I could feel it. I just couldn't trust myself in this area fully after overcoming such horrible, abusive ministry experiences in the past. I was arising in courage and power from a deep healing stream with my local pastors. I wasn't willing to risk another setback. My heart, my mind and my faith couldn't take it.

But in that moment with Dr. Spake (whom I will refer to as Dr. K from this point forward), I sensed Holy Spirit strongly between us. I can only describe this as Holy Spirit descending upon us like a thick cloud. (This would become a norm in our relationship and further confirmation to me that she was my mentor.)

I lowered my eyes in hopes of forcing swelling tears into a still-place. Whatever answer I had planned to give was lost in the shock of her question and this entire supernatural experience.

Breaking the silence, she asked again: *"Tell me, how can I help you?"*

I couldn't keep her waiting. I met her gaze and told her I was alone and stuck, and had been for a long time. I needed assistance in navigating this time in my life... as an apostle, a woman in ministry, and a woman of color. I was at a point of frustration and really wanted to lay everything down and plant myself on a pastoral team at a local church somewhere with my husband and support that vision fully. Things had been extremely difficult for me.

I didn't fit anywhere.

I refused to sell out for a hand up.

I refused to become a clone in a camp.

There was absolutely no way I would put myself into the position of a slave again. It was as if everywhere I turned, I felt like I had to give up my freedom and the vision in me for ministry to move forward. I can remember declaring before the Lord, "I would remain in obscurity FOREVER before I compromise what I know is right for me." In addition, my life craves authenticity and true relationship. I did not want to compromise that and become someone I couldn't face at the end of the day. I was called to the apostolic office in the worship arts by God. Countless apostles affirmed the gift as did my pastor. This wasn't my desire, but it was God's will and who in their right mind would fight against the Lord? Not me.

Yet, at the same time I was in no hurry to do anything about it until other apostles and apostolic leaders began placing a demand on me to receive the fullness of the mantle and walk it out. I am grateful for those leaders who stood with me during this time of ongoing transition and such critical change.

As far as I was concerned, the idea of being an apostle in worship and the arts had become a crushing weight riddled with conflict that was too much for me to bear.

So, as I shared this with Dr. K, she listened intently. **Let me say again, "She LISTENED intently and was genuinely concerned!"** She HEARD me and UNDERSTOOD. I would later learn that she knew what it meant to be an outcast and to make your own way when help eludes you.

Yes, I knew I was to render my cares to the Lord. I knew that I could do all things through Christ. But I also knew that Christ and every one of His apostles had people around them to help in their apostolic journey at some point. Even God enlisted the help of men to fulfill His eternal vision. He didn't need to – but He did.

We can have Christ in our lives to the full and still need different kinds of help along the way!

It is through our relationship with Him that we come to realize just how desperately we need partnership, friendship, wisdom, counsel, affirmation, encouragement and strength for the journey.

I did know that I was no longer in need of discipleship. I did not need another class on leadership, **Ephesians 4:11** ministry or evangelism. I did not need to study how to prepare a sermon, cast out demons or lead people to breakthrough in their lives.

I did not need anyone to teach me how to release miracles, signs and wonders or activate those gifts in me. These things were wonderful during the seasons in which I devoured them as a ready student, but I needed stronger meat! My soul was starving for it. I needed the apostolic in the same way that budding prophets crave prophetic environments.

I NEEDED HELP!

And I knew it could only come by way of INTIMATE apostolic mentoring. I needed the wisdom and guidance of THIS forerunner, Dr. K. I needed the kind of counsel that could reach beyond me and into secrets of the Kingdom!

Our meeting in Starbucks was a turning point. Heaven opened over us.

Later, I would learn that Dr. K was not only a pioneering international apostle whose teachings confront patriarchy in the church and overall church reform; but she is an apostolic scribe at a level I had never witnessed among apostles in my life. She studied the Bible and its background with a wild fervency like I did. She had taken her studies further, and visited the biblical sites internationally that gave life to them. In her apostolic capacity, she had published over thirty books. She was also a techie like me, able to navigate a wide range of desktop publishing and website publishing software.

We had so much in common!

I discovered she was an artist – a painter to be exact. She sketches with ease. She also had an extensive love for worship and acapella singing, of which she dedicated a significant part of her life to traveling with a team. She also plays the keyboard. At every possible turn, God was affirming this relationship, and continues to do so.

She is also *fierce* in the spirit as much as she is gentle. I always say to those I mentor: Don't mistake her gentleness for timidity. You will be cut down in seconds when the anointing rages through her teaching or ministry time! I love it because I have a strong personality and have been referred to in ministry as a *"beast"* when it comes to the Word. I laughed... but it spoke into the tangible authority of the Lord that comes forth from apostolic teaching.

I do not want you to think I am boasting. But this aspect of my journey needs to be shared as it is the reason why I was inspired to write this book. Dr. K contradicted nearly everything I had experienced concerning apostolic mentorship. In addition, she was extremely humble. This is rare for ministers with exploits as significant as hers.

There she was – sitting before me. Dr. K's ministry is saturated in an unusual anointing for healings and miracles. She has performed and witnessed miracles globally in her apostolic ministry that are worthy of feature films, novels and history books.

Yet, she was open to me - a strange woman in her early 40s at the time who had literally stalked her online, chased her across Atlanta, pursued her by email and out of state. (I convinced someone to go to a meeting where she was speaking in California just to remind her how serious I was to have her as a mentor.)

I bought her books and started reading them, registered for her school, and before we ever forged a deeper relationship my mind and heart were already transforming. I would dream (and still do) of the revelation that I glean from her teachings, life and books. This had never happened to me before – EVER. I wasn't just reading, but what I learned seemed to infuse itself into my soul and spirit immediately.

What's even crazier is how it became application to my life. I was so thirsty that my ground just drank what it received, and immediately flourished. Only God appointed assignments can produce results instantaneously!

I also want you to know Dr. K *was not* looking for me!

While crying out to the Lord on the computer (which I mentioned earlier), I stumbled across her ministry on the internet while looking for the search term: "school of the apostles." When I discovered she lived here in Atlanta, I nearly lost my mind! (Of course, that's a euphemism meaning "Theresa" was extremely excited and full of joy.) Then the Lord told me: *"This is your mentor. This is your apostle."* Any hesitancy Dr. K had after all my stalking was going to be met with my persistence. I would be Elisha if I had to chasing Elijah! I am so thankful to the Lord that I drove past my fear of rejection and the potential of embarrassment, and pursued *this mother of my heart.*

I needed ALIGNMENT to move into the next phase of my ministry calling and purpose. I needed NAVIGATION in this new place. I needed a God sent vessel who cared for me and seriously wanted to partner in my destiny.

When the 11 disciples **aligned** with Christ, the chief apostle, and stayed the course, they did greater works than Christ!

When Paul **aligned** with Barnabas, Barnabas led him to Peter, James and John. The course of his life and ministry changed. Paul was catapulted into his apostolic destiny at an *accelerated* pace and depth.

When Timothy **aligned** with Paul, he found stability in his ministry, favor with men and DID NOT WRECK HIS SHIP! Paul would later send him forth apostolically to intervene in the churches.

When Onesimus sought apostolic guidance from Paul, he entered **alignment** and went from a wanted criminal to a profitable, willing servant and friend.

Dorcas was **aligned** with Peter. When she fell dead in the city, even her friends knew that only the Apostle Peter had the authority and access to raise her from the dead. So, they went to him and asked him to come help.

Eutychus was **aligned** with Paul's teachings when he fell asleep, fell out of a window and died. The Apostle Paul walked over and raised him from the dead.

Pentecost came on the heels of the obedience of the apostles to prepare, tarry and wait for it. All who came to the meeting received Holy Spirit because PETER intervened when people questioned the move of God. The apostolic voice followed the sound of the wind and apostolic authority spoke into the move of God... completely **realigning** the hearing of men with the Spirit of God and retaining God's presence in the midst of this historical meeting **(Acts 2)**!

I believe apostolic mentorship, whether temporary or long-term, ushers the people of God into "these kinds" of supernatural experiences and awakenings. I know this is what has happened and continues to happen on my behalf. If you have not experienced this type of power through mentorship, I believe the Lord wants you to know it is available. **I believe the key to accessing it lies in our preparation and response.**

Christ and the apostles are EVIDENCE of these truths. Too many believers miss their day of visitation because they cannot BEHOLD, TARRY OR COMPREHEND what God has placed before them through His people.

Do we really understand that the sons of God are carriers of God's glory?

Do we really grasp that God has chosen certain people for specific functions in the earth?

Don't let familiarity block your blessings and cause these relationships to become common... and ineffective. Listen, I have learned it is not always that the power of God is NOT WITH some apostolic types; rather, it is that those around them *shut down* the power through familiarity and unbelief.

We cannot receive from someone what we cannot see in them. In the following passage, Christ describes this perfectly: **Mark 6:4-5 NIV,** *"Then Christ told them, A prophet is without honor only in his hometown, among his relatives, and in his own household.* ***So, He COULD NOT perform any miracles there,*** *except to lay His hands on a few of the sick and heal them..."*

Whoa! That was an "I can't" for Christ! There was something HE COULD NOT DO! And in this case, He was unable to exercise his apostolic office to the full in an environment where He was only seen as "Mary's son." When I look at Dr. K, myself and other apostolic types who are set aside to mentor others, I cringe when I recognize we ARE INVISIBLE to many of them.

Sometimes, this blindness others have is God's will. We are not meant to be seen by them because they are not our assignments. At other times, which I believe is more common, familiarity is as work or there is a hostility toward us hidden in them. I am thankful to the Lord that I could behold my mentor and that she could behold me. The rudder on my boat was bent and my compass was blurred by fog in the season I met her.

Now, I realize we met at the right time and God led us to one another. I told her once I was GRATEFUL that she was obedient in building the online school and publishing her books on the Internet. Had she not published them, I would NEVER have pulled up "the school of the apostles" on the web so easily.

God truly IS the navigator. But on this ship, in this season, He has mentors and mentees NAVIGATING TOGETHER! This is the picture I have of my mentor and I; and some of those I am mentoring. It is also the hope I have for you in your quest.

Apostolic mentors, in intimate mentoring relationships, can function as **a type of cloud by day and/or a pillar of fire by night** – just as God did for children of Israel; and as Christ was to us in the earth. In no way are we saying people take the place of Christ in our lives. However, WISDOM from those sent to us by God offer a level of protection and navigation that functions as a spiritual compass. These pillars of wisdom GO BEFORE US... making the way straight. They offer needed protection through insight and heavenly counsel. We see it throughout scripture.

How can we move without apostolic counsel?

Proverbs 1:8 NIV, *"Listen,* my son, *to your father's instruction and do not forsake your mother's teaching...."*
Exodus 13:21 NIV says, *"The LORD was going before them in a pillar of cloud by day to lead them on the way, and in a pillar of fire by night to give them light, that they might travel by day and by night."*

Proverbs 13:14 NIV, *"The teaching of the wise is a fountain of life, turning a person from the snares of death."*

Ecclesiastes 4:9-10 NIV, *"Two are better than one, because they have a good return for their labor: If either of them falls down, one can help the other up. **But pity anyone who falls and has no one to help them up.**"*

Proverbs 15:22 NIV, *"Plans fail for lack of counsel, but with many advisers they succeed."*

1 Peter 5:1-3 NIV, *"To the elders among you, I appeal as a fellow elder and a witness of Christ's sufferings who also will share in the glory to be revealed: **Be shepherds of God's flock that is under your care, watching over them — not because you must, but because you are willing,** as God wants you to be; not pursuing dishonest gain, but eager to serve; not lording it over those entrusted to you, but being examples to the flock."*

Proverbs 9:9 ESV, *"Give instruction to a wise man, and he will be still wiser; teach a righteous man, and he will increase in learning."*

...Just as a nursing mother cares for her children, so we cared for you. Because we loved you so much, we were delighted to share with you not only the gospel of God but our lives as well. ~1 Thessalonians 2:8

APOSTOLIC MENTORSHIP

So far, our approach to discussing mentorship has been on the general side. While I've talked about apostolic mentorship, we have not really defined it. Now, however, we are going to put definition to the term.

First, apostolic mentorship is not a SPECIAL KIND of mentorship. It is just a **"different kind"** of mentorship and should be considered as such. I do not want those reading this book to think there is no value in other types of mentoring. The truth is, all types of spiritual mentoring have purpose, function and place in the Kingdom.

It is easy to define how each area fits when we take the time to see them in a practical light through the revealing of God's Word. At this stage in my walk with the Lord, I'm not a person who needs "pastoral" mentorship. In no way does this mean I am better than someone who does. Rather, it indicates that I have moved from the point of a student in this area to a teacher. Think of it this way, I have already been pastored extensively. I graduated into the role of pastoring others some years ago. I don't need equipping in this area again.

Secondly, an apostolic mentor IS NOT necessarily a commissioned apostle or someone who will *ever* become an apostle. The apostolic can reveal itself in several ways. It can speak into a dispensation of grace upon a person's life during their calling as an apostle; operate as a special anointing for a season to complete a specific task; or rest as an anointing upon someone's life to facilitate a purpose.

In other words, a believer can operate as an *apostolic* leader, executing *apostolic* functions in his or her metron. I love to present analogies to make things clearer. So, think of it this way: Many people are prophetic, but not everyone walks in the office of a prophet.

In the same way, many people can be apostolic but not all are apostles. As we discuss apostolic mentorship, we are speaking of apostolic leaders not just those called as apostles.

Thirdly, apostolic mentorship can be found in active, occasional and passive mentoring relationships. It is not limited to one specific area or even a specific type. However, it is important to distinguish *apostolic mentorship* from pastoral mentorship and prophetic mentorship efforts which are often targeted to the spiritual development and growth of babes and emerging leaders. These areas are focused on equipping for service, character development, skills training, etc. They are connected to the foundational "growth and development of believers."

This doesn't mean apostolic mentors are not involved at all levels of equipping because many of them are – especially if they are shepherding a congregation, group or ministry. It means this is not necessarily the primary call, work or focus of apostolic *mentoring*.

As I understand it, apostolic mentoring is focused on identifying and mobilizing efforts to "equip the congregation" in its foundational mandate, mission and purpose. As a result, apostolic mentoring is concerned with ensuring ministry stability and soundness; and providing critical guidance and accountability to move forward in the work.

It is strategy focused, solution centered, results oriented, and concerned with lasting impact and influence to keep the Kingdom of God and its leaders unified, on task and moving forward. **Consider these mentors as military <u>generals</u> in the lives of the leaders whom they mentor.** A general, in this sense, is a commander in the military where the role is to maintain the defense of a nation or a people.

They are concerned with the overall operation of their specific area – ensuring every single element in the region is running smoothly, and on alert from an extremely strategic position. Apostolic mentorship always casts vision and clears up confusion concerning God's eternal purpose within an assignment or mission; and provides the resources, steps and tools to get there.

When you meet your true apostolic mentor, you will see a person who (1) has access to the spiritual dimensions needed by the mentee; (2) is an experienced, mission focused, supernatural navigator; (3) operates in a high measure of spiritual authority and wisdom within their metron; (4) has extreme perception, insight and vision concerning what is the PRESENT will of God; and (5) to help you think and prophesy from a governmental perspective.

Also, an apostolic mentor can be anyone flowing under a strong apostolic anointing and authority in the area where you need help. It can even be in a single area where the help is needed. Again, it DOES NOT MEAN that the person is an apostle or will ever become one.

Finally, I don't want you to see this discussion as an *overspiritualizing* of the role of the apostolic mentor. We must see God has endowed His people with unique abilities and graces by Holy Spirit and empowered them to advance the congregation. As I see it, minimizing this is an affront to the Gospel.

Because of familiarity and a tendency of this generation to look more at one's humanity instead of the mantle upon a person, we can miss what is inside the spiritual mentor. This explanation provides an opportunity to align with the apostolic types around us and honor the Lord in them.

Miracles, signs and wonders are set aside just for the mentee in the lives of the apostolic mentors if they are able to BEHOLD AND RECEIVE THEM without trepidation. I urge you not to take my word for it. Simply study the scriptures to see what happened when the *apostolic* led the way for the people.

I believe we can now define apostolic mentorship as a type of spiritual mentoring that is focused on helping mature believers express, refine and manifest their specific, strategic purpose in the Kingdom. Mentees learn to navigate with extreme precision and clear vision in their specific metron.

Apostolic mentors equip those assigned to them for governmental mastery where faith and belief is uncommon and unwavering.

APOSTOLIC ALIGNMENT

While God has brought tremendous healing in my life and has done a phenomenal work in the ministry entrusted to me, I have faced and will continue to face challenges and struggles. I'll be the first to admit that most of my struggles have been fiercely personal.

Just like all faithful ministers, we will come to a place in which we have this lingering "thorn in the flesh." I have yet to meet a single believer who doesn't have something they have been trying to break free from for years or even decades; or a testimony of overcoming something like this.

Like yesterday, I can remember sitting in my office chair asking the Lord WHEN will this "thorn in the flesh" be taken away!

For a lack of a better word, I learned to live with some things just like our brother Paul and accept that God's grace was sufficient. I continued with the ministry, mentoring, school, family and all the in between with my petition constantly before the Lord.

I was sitting with my mentor one day in a restaurant in North Georgia when the Lord impressed me to tell her about my thorn. He literally whispered to my heart, "You can trust her with this."

For nearly 29 years, I had battled this thorn. All the prayer conferences, inner healing sessions, faith declarations, called fasts, and bottles upon bottles of tears and journaling through the years couldn't take it away. You name the spiritual cure, and I promise you – I tried it.

Outside of my husband and former pastor, no one else was aware of this inward battle. It was shameful to me. To keep our relationship open and to remain accountable, I needed to share it.

Dr. K listened to my one line confession, and then touched my hand. Like a jolt of lightening, the presence of the Lord descended upon us so heavily that time seemed to stop. The atmosphere became so thick and heavy with Holy Spirit that I thought I would succumb to the Lord's power right there on the restaurant floor.

Even the people at the table across from us were experiencing the glory, and it was clear they did not know the Lord. They were gazing at us with that "what in the world is going on" expression as a holy hush rushed through the restaurant. Listen, I know this sounds like an impossible story BUT THIS really happened.

When she touched me, she simply said: "Be healed in Jesus Name!" There was no screaming, stomping, oil throwing... and nothing else. Yet, there we were... weeping and drowning in God's presence. Strangely, when I looked at my phone for the time, hours had passed since we met there for dinner – and we couldn't account for its passing. That was just over two years ago, and to this very day... the thorn has not returned. It was as if the problem never existed.

When I asked the Lord why it took so long for me to be healed, I heard this: "This miracle was sent to help you understand the power of apostolic alignment. This apostle is assigned to this healing and many more in your life to demonstrate my authority and power." And let me tell you, He has.

The Lord used that moment and numerous others to further destroy religious strongholds of performance in my soul. It caused me to grasp a personal revelation and application of the man born blind in John 9. Subconsciously, I thought I had done something to cause or warrant the affliction, this thorn. But in truth, it was put upon me by force. And it was DESTINY that I be released from it in that moment. It would be one of the freeing catalysts that would launch an entirely different ministry in me through the arts – one that speaks into the lives of young girls and women.

Spiritual alignment is the setting of spiritual keys at supernatural points or moments in time that result in a perfect order that literally opens and closes doors to facilitate, accelerate or establish certain moves of God.

Apostolic alignment brings military force! It places you in divine "governmental order" to propel an intentional and strategic design, destiny and purpose that aligns FOUNDATIONS for maximum impact.

When I found my pastors back in 2008 by what seemed like coincidence ... God aligned my heart for healing from a level of brokenness I never thought I could overcome. If I had not followed the Lord's leading and guidance back then, I honestly don't know if I would still be serving Him today or doing anything beyond sitting in a pew in someone's church. My life was IN SHAMBLES. In that instance, I was aligned with pastoral mentors who were healers. That alignment unloosed me into wholeness and opened the gate to walk out my apostolic calling.

Listen, I know there are people who do not believe alignment is needed. For them, it might be true. But I can tell you I believe the planets and the stars in the sky are perfectly aligned under our APOSTOLIC FATHER to facilitate our existence in the earth. What do I mean? I believe it is a picture of all things working in the earth. I have learned that He is always creating opportunities for freedom from confusion, chaos and destruction – not just through the stars (meaning natural navigation), but through people (for spiritual navigation).

ALIGNMENT IS CRITICAL TO NAVIGATION!

In *The Scribal Conservatory* and *The School of the Scribe*, I often receive testimonies from people who speak of what happens when they align with me or the vision God has given me. I share this, not to brag, but to make a point. **When we learn to LIVE APOSTOLICALLY, misaligned, cracked and eroding foundations will be realigned and restored.**

We are so blessed that the God of the Universe desires to work in, with and through us. What a privilege! I am grateful for alignment; and the potential to bring alignment to others through the grace of the apostolic.

Psalm 11:1-4 NIV says, *"In the LORD I take refuge; How can you say to my soul, flee as a bird to your mountain; For, behold, the wicked bend the bow, they make ready their arrow upon the string to shoot in darkness at the upright in heart. If the foundations are destroyed, What can the righteous do?"*

TOO MANY VOICES

This is a tough subject, but it must be addressed.

We live in a time when people are drowning amid a sea of prophetic voices – social media, streaming services, books, audio, etc. For those who hop from buffet to buffet, their spiritual consumption gives birth to extreme confusion, unsound doctrine, religion and twisted doctrinal beliefs.

It breaks my heart to see so many people buy into spiritual lies. So much is released that has absolutely no root in the NOW Gospel. One of my prerequisites for INTIMATE apostolic mentoring relationships is that the mentee commits fully to our mentoring relationship.

This is not control, but protection for the relationship between the mentor-mentee as well as purity around the spiritual deposit in the life of the mentee.

This understanding about "too many voices" can prevent confusion in a person's life. It is very difficult to mentor someone apostolically if they are enrolled in prophetic schools of ministry from multiple sources or if they already have other apostolic or prophetic voices in their ear.

In mentoring relationships in scripture both in Old & New Covenants, there are patterns of mentor and mentee relationships as it relates to spiritual growth and development.

- Christ had the ear of John.

- Moses had the ear of Joshua.

- Naomi had the ear of Ruth.

- Eli had the ear of Samuel.

- Samuel had the ear of Nathan.

- Barnabas had the ear of Paul.

- Mordecai had the ear of Esther.

- Elijah had the ear of Elisha.

- Paul had the ear of Onesimus.

Can you imagine ten prophets trying to intimately train one mentee in the office of the prophet at the same time? I hope not! A mentor can have multiple mentees; but a mentee should not have multiple INTIMATE mentors. They must be cautious regardless of where they may see themselves in their spiritual development.

Intimate mentoring relationships are, well, INTIMATE!

Dedicated mentoring plans are being supernaturally developed to help the mentee be successful – millions of hands can't be on that, shouldn't be on that. INTIMATE apostolic mentors will often teach doctrines that oppose or will uproot what the mentee has previously learned.

Can you imagine being taught one prophetic concept by one current mentor and a conflicting prophetic concept by a different current mentor? At some point, the voice of one of those mentors will rise above the other in your life.

I have worked with people who see me as their apostolic mentor, yet most of the things they teach and post – are born out of books, prophecy lists and teachings from ministers who do not know they exist and would never be available to help them off the ledge or pull a cart down the street!

Where is the impartation of Moses into Joshua? Where is the impartation of Paul into Timothy? Where is the impartation of Mordecai into Esther?

Apostolic mentors are investing THEIR LIVES in THE LIVES of their mentees. They are inviting the MENTEE into the most intimate of archives and spiritual reservoirs. Most of these mentors will not work within man-made chaos and confusion. Not only is this pattern not biblical, but it doesn't hold up within the educational structure of apprenticeship which closely resembles mentorship as we discuss it in this book.

As a mentor and mentee, I know what this is like.

So, when I aligned with Dr. K, I "DECIDED" to become a dedicated student which involved limiting the access of other voices in my spiritual development. People could share with me as friends, but they could not navigate with me in a mentoring capacity.

Remember, apostolic mentoring is about TRANSITIONING a person from one plane of existence into another.

REAL HELP WANTED

Everyone needs help!

What this looks like, however, is as wide and vast as the land across the earth.

Again, a mentor who is actively walking in scribal ministry and the arts, I have gleaned quite a bit from my successes and mistakes in working with people.

Often, I feel as if I've learned more from my mistakes than I have from my success. I've also gleaned tremendously from watching Dr. K's approach with me. What I've learned most is (1) how important it is to keep your heart close to Holy Spirit concerning your mentee and yourself; (2) Keep your soul saturated in God's word; and (3) hold fast to your solid prayer life - always training in *compassion*, high discernment, humility and clarity of mind within yourself as a mentor.

In addition, mentors and mentees MUST KNOW who are assigned to them, and whether it is temporary or long-term. Just because someone asks me to mentor them, doesn't mean I should or that they are my assignment. It's easy to get caught up in a moment.

So, I encourage you to seriously consider the challenges presented to you in this book. While you might not know all your apostolic mentor will contribute to your life, you do need a baseline of expectation that is *saturated* in prayer and wisdom.

Review the interview responses concerning what a serious mentee might expect to find in an apostolic mentor. I believe each one of us can identify something within them that speaks to or has spoken to our journey in seeking help. As you review them, keep in mind there is more to apostolic mentoring than perceived anointing and skill. Look for the practical as well as the spiritual:

Bernard Boulton, a congregational pastor for over 30 years, wrote, *"Transparency: The mentor should be willing to show himself. He should share his scars, his pains and his failures. A mentor establishes credibility when he can be honest about himself.*

Loyalty: A mentor must stand with his student, fight with him and fight for him. He must defend him and cover him when he falls. Will my mentor be with me when everyone else has left me?"

Belinda Beach, a trauma advocate, minister and mentor, wrote, *"A minister must be matured enough to understand the seriousness of a heart being entrusted into their hands. If a mentor is not BOTH mature and able to maintain confidentiality, the mentee becomes prey, subject to emotional blackmail and abuse."*

Terrance Frederick, who oversees a congregation, wrote, *"For me, a mentor needs to be masterful in the Seal (field or metron) I am destined to grow in. By that, I mean they need to be able to see where I am in my apprenticeship (novice, intermediate, master) and customize a strategy for me to get from where I am to where I am supposed to go.*

I actually want them to show out (not in a boastful way but...) in a way that demonstrates confidence that I can trust they 'own' that territory. I want to be able to boast about my mentor not because they are prideful but because they are the real deal. I don't want my mentors to be jealous of me. They have to be broader than my area of specialty."

Andrea Renfroe, a mentor and coach, wrote: *"This is extremely critical for me! A personal ministry mentor must DEMONSTRATE a deep, high and wide relationship with Christ. It sets the foundation from which relationship is built with the mentee. Specifically, it is a reminder of covenant.*

It also provokes the mentee to invest in and treat their relationship with Christ with honor and respect because real relationship is not casual. There is absolutely, positively no way a mentor can properly and accurately lead a mentee without Christ. No way, No how!"

As I see it, these are broad examples of realistic expectations of mentorship, and it explains WHY PEOPLE NEED HELP. In sharing them, I want to reiterate that YOU MUST decide what qualities are essential to you – whether you are choosing active or occasional mentorship. Why? Because they speak into your need and hope for progress, growth and overall success. They speak into the foundation on which you will draw water.

DIFFICULT LESSONS & POOR MENTORS

Also, I want you to consider how unhealthy, unrealistic expectations can impact your life. Be aware, however, that relationships GROW, SHAPE, DEVELOP, HIT ROCKY PLACES OR CHALLENGING TURNS for both the mentee and the mentor. This is expected; and should be handled in Christ's character. To walk into mentoring relationships blindly thinking they will be perfect is ridiculous!

There are no perfect mentors and mentees. All relationships should grow together in Christ.

I sat under abusive leadership riddled in control and manipulation. While I was building my ministry, my "apostolic mentor" was working behind the scenes tearing it down. In my ignorance, I had no idea what was going on until it was in shreds.

Every ounce of confidence and trust I had in leadership and the local congregation went up in flames. Our relationship didn't start out negative. In fact, it was Godly and strong in the beginning. But as I began to emerge from the nest and soar, every possible effort was made to block me in those maturing seasons. I felt like a rebellious teenager fighting a restrictive parent – only I wasn't doing anything but emerging into maturity, finally embracing my identity in Christ and walking out my calling.

I know it's easy to play the victim and blame others for our hurt, but this testimony is not that. I have not been very outspoken about what I endured and how things ended. I let gossip have its way, and chose to let people believe whatever they wanted. My healing process took YEARS! The things I was subjected to near the end of that relationship in secret were appalling, and only God and I know the depth of that truth.

I nearly lost my mind as I fought grief, depression, spiritual confusion, offense, unforgiveness and even suicide. **A horrible mentoring relationship brought me to this point.** Again, sometimes things that start out ordained of God can go extremely wrong.

For years, the mere mention of apostolic covering, mentoring, mothering or fathering turned my stomach and sent a fear all through me. But what I learned is now directed in helping others. Blessed be the Lord of all comfort. I have strong apostolic mentoring and leadership now that represents the Father's heart in this area.

There can be "hard places" in mentoring relationships; and there can also be "abusive places." We must be *diligent* in avoiding the latter – and both mentor and mentee play joint roles in understanding that. Mentees can be abusive too!

One of the most profound responses I received came from Frederick. He wrote about the mistakes he made in choosing a mentor: *"I went after skill alone and did not check to see if personalities matched. I looked for another parent in the faith instead of a mentor. I had the wrong expectations not because the mentor was not competent, but we were at different stages, and it was not compatible. The Mentor was not accessible, and they were already spread too thin. I felt like I was being hustled and it was too commercial. Everything had a price attached, but the mentor did not know that though I wasn't rich, I had so much admiration for them that I was willing to volunteer and meet needs that the mentor was lacking in their program and make up for the money I could not pay to take the classes. They were looking to land big sharks and I was just a budding fish.*

"Mentors need to be able to see how open the apprentice is to them as individuals, because they need to determine if this is just another student or someone who will add to my mentorship program as it expands. To this day my admiration is still great for their vast knowledge and wisdom, but I still see gaps in that mentor that I would have been able to help fix, if I was not just looked at as another dollar."

Boulton wrote this in response to choosing the wrong mentor, *"I once chose the wrong mentor because I was hungry for one. Never choose a mentor when you're desperate! I was in a drought spiritually and this person came to me and prophesied to me, and I was hooked.*

When the thrill was gone, I knew I had made a mistake. He tried to control me and when I pulled back his feelings got hurt. I discovered that he couldn't mentor me, and I really needed to be his mentor. The right (apostolic) mentor will have impact. They will be a role model and a pioneer."

It is time to go deeper.

So, Elijah went from there and found Elisha son of Shaphat. He was plowing with twelve yoke of oxen, and he himself was driving the twelfth pair. Elijah went up to him and threw his cloak around him. Elisha then left his oxen and ran after Elijah. Let me kiss my father and mother goodbye, he said, "and then I will come with you." ~1 Kings 19:19-20

AM I READY FOR AN APOSTOLIC MENTOR?

I am convinced only a few people within our communities are ready for an apostolic mentor on an INTIMATE level. When you hear the word INTIMATE or INTIMACY, I want you to think "in your face" mentorship – the drill sergeant and the private; the law enforcement major and the cadet/rookie; or the diligent parent and the son. I am NOT speaking of the yelling, pointing in the face or those known militant behaviors, but the *intensity* and dedication to the equipping. I want you to consider the kind of mentorship that invades every aspect of your life – in the name of LOVE.

Paul said this to Timothy, *"I am reminded of your sincere faith, which first dwelt in your grandmother Lois and your mother Eunice, and I am convinced that it is in you as well."* **(2 Timothy 1:5 NIV)**

In the book of Acts, we learn that Paul heard about Timothy the evangelist's outstanding reputation during one of his missionary journeys. Reputation was a BIG DEAL in Biblical times and in Hebrew culture. A good name was coveted greater than any type of wealth or riches. So, to see scripture refer to Timothy's reputation isn't a small mention. More than likely, it meant Timothy was not only well-respected and honored by those who knew him, but he was also well-known or popular among some of the believers.

Further, **2 Timothy 1** reveals that Paul was a witness to Timothy's sincerity and faith in the Lord. We know he knew Timothy's grandmother and mother. They were strong, faithful servants in the Lord who had already raised Timothy in the knowledge of Christ.

What is shocking, however, is some scholars speculate that Timothy was a teenager when he first encountered Paul (**2 Timothy 4:12).** Scholars also believe Christ's apostles were teenagers except for Peter. Given Jewish culture, this is more likely than not.

We learn that Timothy was of mixed race – both Jew and Greek, and at some point, he became Paul's protégé. Paul referred to him as a son in the Lord and would send him out on "apostolic" assignments.

As an apostolic mentor, mentees can obtain a level of intimacy similar to what existed between Timothy and Paul. There was authentic relationship, mutual respect, love and a heart for Christ's work. Paul didn't just know Timothy, but he knew his family, spiritual inheritance and could see his potential. He also showed authentic interest in Timothy's background and upbringing. From this we can see intimate apostolic mentorship is not focused on one area of a person's life, but the totality of who the person is – past, present and future.

From their relationship, we can also see you do not have to be a baby in the Lord to have a mentor. Timothy was not a proselyte in the faith, but advanced and mature in his knowledge of Christ and was already doing the work. So, when he came under the mentorship of Paul, he had all the necessary pieces in place for refining through apostolic mentorship.

Lao Tzu said, "When the student is ready the teacher will appear. When the student is truly ready... The teacher will disappear."[1] This famous quote implies that:

---

[1] Maria Pellicano, "The Art of Powerful Communication: Aligning your mindset, mission and voice," (Pellicano Creative Consulting: 2016), Victoria Melbourne, 63.

- The student is prepared mentally, emotionally and spiritually to receive the mentor.

- The student is holistically ready to move forward.

- The student is at the cusp of transitioning into greater.

- The student is humble and teachable.

- The student will build upon the foundation of the teacher, excel and do greater works.

- The student will become a teacher.

The teacher or mentor will phase out his role as a mentor, and enter a deeper relationship with the student on another level. Thus, the teacher disappears. We see this with God and Abraham; and Christ and his disciples.

The result of mentorship is always multiplication, expansion in the Kingdom and friendship **(Genesis 1:28, 9:7; 2 Timothy 2:1-3)**. What does this mean? It means that the goal of the mentor is to multiply an aspect of his or her supernatural man in some form in the life of the person they are mentoring.

Paul declared this in **1 Corinthians 11:1 NIV**, *"Be imitators of __ME__ as I am in Christ."*

For a mentee to receive apostolic mentorship on an INTIMATE level, they must posture themselves – even in their maturity – **TO IMITATE** the heart, the message and the power executed by their mentor. Do not be paranoid here and worried about losing yourself. God would NEVER allow you to become a copycat under STRONG apostolic leadership. But it is an HONOR to mirror the Christ in your mentor!

THE APOSTOLIC MIND

To fully appreciate and apprehend the value, depth, power and significance of apostolic mentoring, the mentee must come to recognize, know and understand the "apostolic mind." Please note I am not speaking of a "mind-set," which deals with an established set of attitudes people accumulate through knowledge and experience.

The apostolic mind as the Lord has shown me is completely different from what I believe would be considered a mind-set. The difference is men can manipulate mind-sets, but the "apostolic mind" belongs to God... because it is God in us. This premise is the foundation for everything we teach within "The Sealed School of Ministry," where we learn that the Ephesians 4:11 gifts are seals of God's character and heart for humanity, and each person who is endowed with one of these seals must present themselves as letters before men... with seals meant to be broken.

Therefore, the apostolic mind is the mind of God operating THROUGH MANKIND to release His character and heart for humanity **(Mark 12: 30-31)**. Collectively, these seals ripped the veil, shook the foundations, caused the dead to rise and walk the earth, etc. after the resurrection. It is the LOVE OF GOD FOR A PEOPLE CALLED TO HIMSELF that propels HIS MIND. I believe the apostolic mind of God is exemplified **FULLY** through the **GIFT** of the "mind of Christ." The fruit of the spirit is at the core of this mind.

The mind of Christ is perpetually pushing us into the reality of God's heart for reconciliation. The apostolic mind is the KEY to establishing the purest of understandings concerning the "FINISHED WORK" of Christ. Without it, we will miss the heartbeat of INTIMATE apostolic mentoring as it is shared in this book.

We miss this truth: GOD IS FOCUSED ON IN WITH US NOT CASUAL RELATIONSHIP!

Philippians 2:5-8 KJV says, *"__Let THIS MIND be in you,__ which was also in Christ: Who, being in the form of God, thought it not robbery to be equal with God: But made himself of no reputation, and took upon Him the form of a servant, and was made in the likeness of men: And being found in fashion as a man, He humbled himself, and became obedient unto death, even the death of the cross."*

1 Corinthians 16:2b NIV, *"...But __WE HAVE__ the mind of Christ."*

HIS mind is not unstable!

The "apostolic mind" operates out of a military framework. It is constantly concerned with preparation, strategy, alignment, formation, mobilization and execution. Every ounce of supernatural sight comes from the aerial perspective.

At all times, the apostolic mind is thinking and moving in these terms in the hopes of bringing forth solutions and conclusions to problems. This is COMPLETELY DIFFERENT from the focus of the prophetic mind, the pastoral mind or the evangelistic mind which has goals and outcomes specific to their realm that are needed and necessary.

A person who is not prepared for "apostolic-minded" leadership might perceive apostolic responses or directives as harsh, lacking compassion, forceful or disagreeable. In reality, it is the thrust of the apostolic that seeks to put away those things that can stifle, block or hinder progress and clear the way for eagle's eye vision. The apostolic knows how to move people out of emotionalism.

One of the most profound examples of the apostolic mind can be seen in God's response to Job.

He said to him, "Pull up your pants Job... or be a man!"

The apostolic mind will not allow a person to be ORDINARY, or limited in their humanity. It pulls them out of self-focus into mission focus – regardless of the circumstances. It raises them up to manifest the GODLINESS on the inside of them.

The apostolic mind understands how to move beyond the cares of this world into purpose so the army can advance. What if Paul had focused on being in prison? Would the wisdom in the letters to the churches have come forth? What if Stephen had focused on his pain? Would he have seen the Christ in his last moments? What if Christ had focused only on what He was about to endure? Would He have made it out of the Garden of Gethsemane? By recognizing, acknowledging and understanding the apostolic mind, quite a bit of unnecessary hurt feelings and emotional confusion can be AVOIDED in mentoring relationships.

Mentees need to know what they are asking for when they SEEK OUT AN INTIMATE APOSTOLIC MENTOR!

For some apostolic mentors, especially those who are apostles, the apostolic is a LIFESTYLE! Understanding these realities about the apostolic will end a lot of confusion concerning apostolic mentorship and heal broken relationships.

How is this possible? Well, when we know how a thing operates and what it looks like... we are less likely to misinterpret or misunderstand the function. The apostolic mind is a powerful gift released to us in our dominion and calling.

The apostolic mind is not an emotional, weepy mind. It doesn't vacillate on indecisiveness, mood swings and shifting attitudes. This doesn't mean people don't have trouble. But it does mean they won't LIVE in their trouble. Coming into the "apostolic mind" is the most STABLE ministry ascension in all the scriptures. Is it founded on **THE ROCK!** Isn't the apostolic a part of the FOUNDATION? Foundations DO NOT SHIFT AND MOVE LIKE SAND AND WIND!

The scripture tells us Christ wept. Then it was over! The scripture tells us Christ sweat blood and cried out in agony for God to take His cup away. When God didn't, Christ stopped crying, wiped the bloody sweat from His face and immediately accepted his apostolic transition! **Christ optimized His "apostolic mind" in the Garden of Gethsemane... and never shifted away from that higher place again. HIS NEW MAN EMERGED WITH GREATER FORCE AND PURPOSE!**

I am desperate for readers to get this specific revelation. The mind of Christ isn't a baseball cap we can put on in times of trouble and at every random prayer; and then take off.

It is a permanent mind transformation! In my own life, it was like the ultimate ugly break-up – walking away from a person I knew a long time ago who was unprofitable for me for the final time. Only the person was me, and I was completely done with her.

It is impossible for the **apostolic mind** to live between the prophetic and emotionalism. Having emotions and being emotional are two very different things! The apostolic mind cries out for the prophetic *within* the apostolic. **Ephesians 4:17-32** speaks to this kind of alignment.

Because the mind of Christ IS THE APOSTOLIC MIND OF GOD, it will LOCK ON TO ALL TARGETS from a military stance. It will respond in a military manner. It will contemplate, strategize and act from a military posture. It is always "thinking like" Christ because it is Christ IN US. The apostolic mind does not understand UNBELIEF!

While it can visualize all possible angles at different levels, the apostolic mind will always choose the higher, most efficient perspective. There is no turning back from this place for those who manage to cross into it. The old has TRULY passed away and all things have become new. A completely new man has come forth! This should give new meaning to passages like "so as a man thinketh so is he" or "put on the mind of Christ."

It can be difficult for some mentees who knew their mentors before or in between their transition into the apostolic mind to adjust to the person emerging or who has emerged. Man have I experienced this! They may resist the transition, and complain that their apostolic mentors have changed. They will look through familiar eyes and pray for the old man to return. Sadly, they are unable to see what is or has truly taken place in the spirit. If unchecked, resentment will sweep in.

When mentees try to relate to their mentor through an old or cloudy lens, they do so with familiarity. They become completely incapable of tapping into the apostolic.

Instead of seeking to understand God's way and ascend into a new place, they lower themselves into the mind of man saturated in familiarity, unable to see outside of their own needs and personal judgments. EXTREME agitation and tension can emerge between the mentor and the mentee. The level of frustration there can be relationship-breaking as the mentees unrenewed mind meets the apostolic mind head on – and they collide in negativity.

As a result, mentees can feel left behind, abandoned or overlooked as the apostolic work seems to continue without them. The apostolic mentor, however, longs to see the mentee enter the change but only Holy Spirit can usher them in through a contrite heart, not a bitter and closed one. **The mentee must realize that the old man is being ripped away from them amid the ascension of the apostolic mentor.**

Most mentees miss this and leave in anger before their transition is complete. Sometimes, leaders must release mentees from their tutelage, place them with another mentor or encourage them to find one on their own. Otherwise, they can quickly become the mentor's adversary or enemy.

There are people whom I mentored who grew to despise me because of this. I "changed" on them or rather, I ascended deeper into the apostolic mind. How many leaders are in this position right now? How many have had to let go of mentees because those mentees did not understand the mentoring process? Could more communication or greater explanation have saved the relationship or was it inevitable that it turn out this way? I do know this: God wants fruitfulness.

Apostolic mentors cannot be forced into old seasons by anyone... as the "mind of Christ" in them has become and continues to become a divine, strategic missile for the Kingdom. Through them, certain types of miracles, signs, wonders and releases are only loosed by divine apostolic alignment.

Don't be so quick to throw your mentor away when disagreement happens. True relationship is always tested. But the beauty of INTIMACY is that you work it out, and grow together when both parties submit to forgiveness, embrace humility, accept their respective roles in the relationship and CHOOSE to work through the dark times.

Intimate relationship is an investment in COVENANT, and in the love of God. Learn to endure and increase your capacity to love. This posture is critical to impartation! I firmly believe insight into the apostolic mind is critical to embracing apostolic mentorship. It ensures you are better prepared to learn the way of the apostolic.

Don't miss your day of visitation!

Luke 9:1 NIV, *"When Christ had called the Twelve together, HE GAVE THEM POWER..."*

Up to this point, Christ had poured heavily into those under his mentorship. We already know from **John 17** He didn't withhold anything profitable for their growth, development and success.

So, when we consider this statement in Luke, I want you to consider it from this perspective:

1. The disciples were READY to receive power when He gathered them together.

2. Christ more than likely laid hands on them and/or anointed them.

3. This POWER was tangible, meaning it could be experienced or observed through demonstration.

4. This POWER came with direct authority to "accomplish" a specific task. In this instance, they were given power and authority to tread upon serpents and scorpions...

5. This POWER was destined to bring a release from bondage. It was a TRAMPLING power! To thread means to crush, stomp or level... as in take victory over.

Remember, we are imitators of Christ in the earth. Our apostolic mentors have Christ's apostolic authority within their measure to IMPART AND RELEASE from the apostolic mind!

Since my alignment with Dr. K, my confidence in the apostolic is through the roof (in a healthy, humble way of course)! I have increased in POWER and in AUTHORITY within my metron. I can feel it, see it... and so can others around me. When I travel, I've seen a stronger opposition than I have ever experienced in my spiritual life. Yet, I am completely equipped with the "apostolic mind" to TRAMPLE the serpent and scorpion... and escape unscathed.

Again, I am not bragging on a person just to boast.

My hope is to bring us, as a people, back into the reality of the "spiritual bond" that comes by way of mentorship and apostolic grace.

We have become so COMMON to one another among the body that we are BLIND to the power God sends in our midst. **We should desire and be able to behold the LIVING GOD inside one another!** We have allowed our "supernatural relationships" to rest in familiar fields.

As mentors, not only do we want to be able to SEE what God has placed in our mentees; but we also want those we mentor to see what God has placed in us. Reciprocity is always necessary.

When we posture ourselves correctly, it permeates every aspect of our lives – not just one area.

Listen, I know I have received POWER from Dr. K! Just like Timothy knew he received from Paul and became a son. How can a general in a military formation release anything less than POWER? The core of the apostolic is centered on going, doing and having impact.

On numerous occasions, Christ sent his disciples in peace as the Father sent Him. And in the instance below, we see He "breathed on them" and then prophesied to them.

Christ released certain anointings only on those He mentored intimately. This is indisputable. It means our apostolic mentors can do the same within their realm of authority.

John 20:20-22 ESV, *"Jesus said to them (his disciples)* ***PEACE BE WITH YOU.*** *As the Father has sent me, even so I am sending you. And when He had said this,* ***HE BREATHED ON THEM*** *and said to them, Receive the Holy Spirit..."*

The standard is always before us:

o Our Father is the standard and set the standard.
o Christ imitates the standard of the Father.
o The disciples imitated the standard Christ.

The Apostle Paul declared this to those intimate with him: "Imitate me as I imitate Christ." I do the same within the boundaries of the ministry entrusted to me.

RESPECT & HONOR

Compared to my apostolic mentor, I am young in walking out my calling in the apostolic. I make no claim to having an extensive understanding of the prophetic or the apostolic. But the portion I do have has saved my life as we look at the pomp and circumstance that shapes many of the ideas on mentorship today. I know the Lord has given me a portion to add to this conversation.

When we consider INTIMATE mentorship, we must grasp that we are asking someone to use their life, experiences, wisdom, knowledge and understanding to TEACH US. For the apostolic mentor, it is like asking someone to hold "college or university studies with you" one-on-one. The primary difference is instead of being herded into a classroom, you are being invited into the privacy of a person's bedroom. I use this description because the bedroom is the most intimate place in the home for most people. Even Christ invites us into the bridegroom's chamber.

This is a BIG DEAL! No one must serve this way!

Dr. Spake's journey begs of my honor and respect. And guess what, so does the journey of your INTIMATE apostolic mentor, whether you are in relationship now or it is on the way.

Consider this the perfect time to determine where your heart rests as you prepare to embrace your mentor. Paul said in his own words in **1 Corinthians 15:9** that "he was the **least** of the apostles" when he looked at those who were around him. Then, he shares the reasons why prior to and immediately after making this statement. He understood honor.

In some mentoring relationships, the mentor may be younger and the mentee older in years. There is absolutely NOTHING wrong with this AS LONG AS respect and honor stand at the center.

I have mentored people twice my age! But understand, I stayed IN MY LANE in respect to that and preserved their dignity. While I may have spiritual food for them, I must still honor their eldership and experience!

Paul acknowledged his "low rank or stature" in his assessment in **1 Corinthians 15.** This wasn't a demoralizing statement but one in which he is able to see himself in a correct light, and states his place and his role among them. He did not think more highly of himself than he ought. In his time, the original apostles and other apostolic types including Paul *were famous* and walking out the newness of Christ's legacy.

His position here blessed me because it speaks boldly into humility, honor and respect for those who are pioneering today. I beg you: Honoring someone is not about them being BETTER THAN OR GREATER THAN. This perspective presents a *small* view of God in the hearts of men.

Paul's apostolic mantle was a direct result of God's release of the apostolic office into the earth through the original apostles, and the continuous demonstration of the office. Paul recognized and understood he was standing on the shoulders of giants, and would one day become a giant in the faith himself.

Yet, he didn't worship them or idolize them! We should stand in this place also among our apostolic mentors.

To me, Dr. K is a giant!

Romans 13:7 NIV states, *"Give to everyone what YOU OWE THEM: If you owe taxes, pay taxes; if revenue, then revenue;* **if respect, then respect; if honor, then honor."** *This is the way of the Gospel. Period. Let us be the generation that reclaims and restores it.*

1 Peter 2:17 NKJV states, *"Honor all people. Love the brotherhood. Fear God. Honor the king."*

1 Thessalonians 5:12-13 NIV, *"Now we ask you, brothers and sisters, to acknowledge those who work hard among you, who care for you in the Lord and who admonish you.* ___Hold them in the highest regard in love___ *because of their work. Live in peace with each other."*

- God should not become common to His people.
- Christ should not become common to His people.
- Those sent to lead and guide in a spiritual capacity should not become COMMON to those to whom they are assigned.

INTIMATE mentorship is a special gift from God! COVET IT!

It should be noted that time and experience are not always reflective of maturity. I have met people who claim apostolic authority and have been saved triple the time than I have but are babes in their understanding of weighty things. Your mentor should be SKILLED and REVELATORY in your specific area above where you are. We cannot be deceived by "time and experience" alone.

BE OPEN TO CORRECTION

Proverbs 1:7 NIV, *"The fear of the LORD is the beginning of knowledge, but fools despise wisdom and instruction."*

Don't be a fool.

Years ago, one of the house parents in the children's group home where I grew up spoke this phrase often. It wasn't said in a condescending, demeaning manner, but in the same way that a parent might say to their child, "Daughter, listen." It was an endearing expression to reject ignorant behavior and attitudes.

Correction is a part of wisdom and instruction. Correction is the act of rectifying or redefining something previously identified as an error or mistake. Correction is the act of making something better than it was before, not tearing it down. I am convinced that no human being can live or walk this earth in wisdom without correction THROUGHOUT their lives – not just at certain points.

Prophetic people should be open to correction from natural and spiritual perspectives FROM THEIR INTIMATE MENTOR. It's funny how we understand this in the workplace and in our efforts as creative artists, but we don't quite grasp it concerning issues of spiritual development. The more I work with people who claim they want mentorship, the more I realize they really want a buddy who offers occasional advice and insight.

A mentor who is unable to bring correction to his mentee IS NOT A MENTOR, but a member of a fan club. Correction is not optional, but required. Would a private fight against the wisdom and instruction of the general? Would a cadet or rookie fight against the wisdom and instruction of the law enforcement captain?

This is a question every mentee should answer in INTIMATE apostolic mentorship. The heartbeat of mentoring is centered on proper alignment.

RECEIVE THE PROPHETIC WORD
FROM YOUR MENTOR

A mentee called me one day in need of advice about an extremely serious situation. They even opened the conversation like this: "I need a Word from the Lord concerning what I should do here. Will you help me?" Let me tell you, I heard from Heaven concerning their request and delivered an extremely accurate word of direction, instruction and prophetic insight.

Then the mentee said, "I will pray about it and see what the Lord says." This statement frustrated me intensely as an INTIMATE apostolic mentor. Why? Because the mentee failed to recognize God had already answered. How can a person have prophetic counsel from an apostolic mentor and then REFUSE to accept the counsel?

A mentee should be able to trust the prophetic word from their INTIMATE mentor.

I was still in the process of pursuing Dr. K when I registered to attend a women's conference she was hosting. Our relationship was extremely new, and she had not decided to take me on as a mentee at this point. Like I shared previously, I "STILL KNEW" she was my apostle and mentor. In the last session of the conference, Dr. K began to prophesy to me.

She said, "You are doing too many things. To move forward, you must choose the School of the Scribe, the Literary Ministry or these other things you are doing – but you cannot do all of them."

Immediately, I understood what that Word meant. On my way home from the conference I called an emergency meeting with those in my ministry.

On the call, I announced I was shutting down Voices of Christ Literary Ministries International after 14 years, and focusing all of my attention on The School of the Scribe. I released them from any obligations to the ministry and asked them to pray with me concerning next steps in the coming months. The next day, I began the administrative process.

I made it clear that I wasn't letting them go, but letting go of the ministry – as it was a dead seed.

I had to TRUST that I had heard the Lord concerning Dr. K! I had to believe she held the insight and wisdom into my apostolic destiny from the Lord that I needed. I had to hear her from an APOSTOLIC MIND – not from the mind of "Theresa."

I didn't go home to pray. Why? Because my very cry for a mentor was for someone who could help me NAVIGATE! Her instruction fit within my cry from the Lord. There is a PROPHETIC and REVELATORY dimension to apostolic mentorship. The example I shared here was TRULY revelatory.

Mentees must learn to trust the prophetic word from the Lord in their mentors AND RESPECT THE WORD! I know that is a stern statement, but the evidence of biblical mentoring relationships supports it. Did not Elijah say it was going to rain? Did not Moses prophesy that the Lord would rescue the children of Israel from Pharaoh?

There are so many scriptural examples of MENTEES responding correctly to their APOSTOLIC MENTORS and receiving immediate breakthrough as a result.

I am only able to write this book and move in ministry at the level I am now because I ACTIVATED THE PROPHETIC WORD from the vessel assigned to me.

If you cannot trust the prophetic word from your mentor, then your mentor really can't help you! Again, this is not an attempt to cause you to follow someone blindly, but rather a declaration for the mentee to ask the Lord to give him or her a heart to recognize GOD in the mentor.

DISAGREEMENT IS INEVITABLE

Doctrinal disagreement is inevitable between mentors and mentees. How disagreement is viewed and handled is what matters most.

I have served under and alongside leaders who took offense to any form of disagreement. This is extremely unhealthy. To not agree, in some situations, can be equivalent to an act of rebellion, dissent and the inciting of strange war.

This is so contrary to what Christ taught and the examples we see among the apostles. As many of us know, disagreement isn't necessarily negative. Different opinions do not always mean "wrong." It simply means that varying perspectives exist.

I urge you to learn what doctrines (or even denominational differences) are critical to your belief system prior to entering INTIMATE relationship with a mentor. Discuss them in detail. You want to make sure there are no deal breakers. Where there are differences you want to discuss them and find common ground if possible. Failing to establish doctrinal foundations early within your mentoring relationship can result in extreme conflict later.

From the very beginning Dr. K said this to me: "Theresa, it is okay to have a different opinion or perspective. We do not have to agree, because there should be room for different perspectives."

Me? Blank stare. Seriously.

She caught me off guard again. Why? Because I have never had an apostolic mentor say such a thing to me. In fact, I have not always been a mentor who was at ease with different opinions. I had to GROW INTO understanding this. I grew up "old school" in the faith.

In my own life, for example, varying views concerning the end-times are not deal breakers for me. I'm too busy living in the NOW to worry about the end. So, pre-or-post tribulation discussions are non-issues. I have no problem discussing them or listening to different perspectives. Whatever my mentor's or mentees' perspective may be on this subject does not impact our relationship.

This discussion is critical. I know of Godly relationships that have gone up in flames because of doctrinal differences. Frankly, if you study the history of the Church, you will learn it was bitter disagreements over doctrine that split it in the first place! And guess what, people are still FIGHTING over these things today with absolutely no resolution. Let us learn to reason together and cast aside those things that do not give life.

Romans 14:19 AMP, *"So let us then definitely aim for and eagerly pursue what makes for harmony and for mutual upbuilding (edification and development) of one another."*

"Be dressed for action and have your lamps lit, like people waiting for their master's return after a wedding feast; so that when He comes and knocks, they will open the door for him without delay. ~ Luke 12:35-36

PREPARE FOR YOUR APOSTOLIC MENTOR

I thank God, I was prepared for my apostolic mentor.

When I look back at my apostolic journey, I realize I've been in preparation for receiving Dr. K for a long time, and my cries for help had never fallen on deaf ears.

This time… and I mean THIS TIME, I didn't miss my visitation. I submitted to the CLEAN UP in my heart and mind, and gained wisdom concerning the power of endurance and patience – even though I struggled to stand. Then, when the circumstances and timing aligned, we met.

I want to say this again: *"I was ready for my mentor."* I have never wanted the "stuff" of our relationship – her connections, in roads, popularity, etc. I have only wanted the portion I believe God has promised me – covenant, friendship, trust, wisdom, revelation, help, etc. Everything else is a tremendous benefit and a blessing. I've only wanted to give those things back in return. In my entire walk with the Lord, I have always been faithful to whomever I was sent.

Only once in my life as a believer has a relationship with a mentor ended horribly. I've never disappeared on a leader or just vanished outside of that incident. It is important to have a track record of commitment and faithfulness in this area.

Dr. K was no different in our connection. My posture is to RECEIVE, PROPERLY DIGEST, EXPAND & GIVE BACK to her – not to take and take. A true mentee must have his or her heart prepared and motives RIGHT as well. Because of this, I can see why God may have waited to make this connection. New wine requires new skin.

Sometimes, we do not really know where we are spiritually until God begins snatching those walls away.

My argument: God prepares mentees for their mentors just like the disciples Christ chose were prepared for Him. At one time, Christ had seventy disciples who seemed like they would remain with Him. But at the end of the day, only a part of the remnant remained. With Dr. K, I decided to be a remnant. You should decide to do the same!

MENTORING CATEGORIES & TYPES

Paul D. Stanley and J. Robert Clinton identified three mentoring categories in their book, *"Connecting: The Mentoring Relationships You Need to Succeed in Life."*

They identified:

Active Mentoring Relationships. In active mentoring relationships multiplication is deliberate or intentional. Types of mentors that fall in this category are: disciplers, who focus on the basics of following Christ; spiritual guides, who provide accountability, direction and insight for decision making; and coaches, who provide motivation, skills training and application to meet tasks.[2]

Occasional Mentoring Relationships. In occasional mentoring relationships, there is a less deliberate approach. Types of mentors that fall in this category are counselors who offer timely advice on viewing self, others, circumstances and ministry; teachers who provide knowledge and understanding on a topic; and sponsors who provide career guidance and development within an organization.[3]

---

[2] Paul D. Stanley and J. Robert Clinton, "Connecting: The Mentoring Relationships You Need to Succeed in Life," (Colorado Springs: NavPress, 1992), Accessed August 29, 2017, http://www.dts.edu/download/campus/internships/DTS-SFL-Mentoring%20Types%20by%20Stanley%20and%20Clinton.pdf
[3] Ibid.

Passive Mentoring Relationships. Passive mentoring is casual. It is a type of mentoring in which a person can learn from someone living or dead whose life inspires emulation,[4] like through a book, streaming media, etc.

I found the insight of Stanley and Clinton invaluable to my focus in this book. Clearly, I could categorize a mentoring relationship that I have as the spiritual guide type in the *active mentoring* category. For many reasons, it is exactly where my mentorship with Dr. K fits! As time passes, it has revealed itself to be MUCH MORE than what "I THOUGHT" I needed.

My challenge to you is to sit before the Lord and decide what category of mentoring relationship fits where YOU ARE, not where you hope to be. Look at what you really need versus. what you want?

Determine what you would like a mentor to impart into your life and at what level? Are you currently looking for active, occasional or passive mentorship? In fact, jot this down before reading through the next few sections.

Define your mentorship expectations. Write them out. Are they realistic and reasonable? How much responsibility do you have in honoring a mentoring relationship? What are you willing to give, to release, to share, etc.?

Are you ready to be taught BEYOND confirmation? Are you ready to be corrected, refined and aligned? Decide how much you are willing to invest in relationship building. Finally, I want to make one more observation from my experiences as a mentee and a mentor.

---

[4] Ibid.

ACTIVE MENTORING isn't just about you, especially when you are enlisting the help of a spiritual guide! Don't be SELFISH! (For those who may be uncomfortable with the phrase spiritual guide, please know it is referring to an intimate level of relationship in which you are seeking spiritual guidance from a sold-out believer of Christ.)

If someone is investing significant time in your life and ministry then the relationship should be seen from a place of mutuality and support. What do I mean? It means you should come into that relationship DETERMINED to be as much of a blessing to that mentor as they are to you. It should not be grievous for you to give back – time, resources and/or money. It should be a joy to bless your mentor. Anything less is prostitution.

2 Timothy 5:18-20 CJB says, *"The leaders who lead well should be considered worthy of **DOUBLE HONOR**, <u>**especially those working hard at communicating the Word and at teaching.**</u> For the Tanakh says, <u>**you are not to muzzle an ox when it is treading out the grain,**</u> in other words, <u>**"The worker deserves his wages.**</u> Never listen to any accusation against a leader unless it is supported by two or three witnesses. Rebuke before the whole assembly those leaders who continue sinning, as a warning to the others."*

This is a "financial scripture." WAGES mean money!

Years ago, I was a part of this apostolic school and network that promised to help me as a minister. I would attend these meetings, sow these seeds, take classes… but never, ever had a chance to get personal questions answered.

There is this illusionary realm that much of the church exists in that says, "God will give you everything you need?" He does, but often He uses people to GIVE TO YOU. Truly, we are "blessed to be a blessing."

The problem, as I have come to see it, is that mentors can sometimes fail to recognize THEIR ROLE in the intimate "giving realm." The people sitting in the pews are not the only ones missing the mark with God's people.

Yet, at each of these meetings, people were making financial pledges into a "system" that, to be honest, had little return in their lives. Even though I was paying to attend the school, we had to buy all these books separately. I would go to meetings and people were seated by giving levels. When it came time for prophecy, the big money got the prophecy first; and those with the two-mites got the prophets in training. This is horrible when people are hurting, and already sacrificing so greatly just to get there.

Listen, CHRIST WOULD NOT IGNORE THIS. He would not send people back into the street to forage for something to give just so they could gain a release from a prophet.

Never had I seen the "life of the Pharisees and hirelings" played out so well in such an organized setting. This was wrong! These meetings were filled with pimps and prostitutes. Period. I cannot apologize for this statement because eyes need to be opened to the reality of Christ or the lack thereof **(2 Timothy 3:1-9).**

What does a "worthy leader" look like to you? It's time to distinguish between shepherds and hirelings, worthy and unworthy leaders **(2 Timothy 5:18-20).**

The operation of a prophetic gift is NOT evidence of God's power or proof that a person is a son. Christ made it clear that we would know who belonged to God BY THEIR LOVE, how they treat the brethren. This IS our line in the sand. Declare that you will not be prostituted!

At the same time, declare that you will not prostitute your INTIMATE apostolic mentor! Leaders who give selflessly are precious to the Lord. Just as you need spiritual food, they need your seed for their livelihood. They need you to understand that your seed activates the gifts in them FOR you. It is the mentees good pleasure to GIVE.

When they pray and ask the Lord to provide, *recognize* that you might be the answer to that prayer. You are the *provision* the Lord made.

What are you willing to give FINANCIALLY to your mentor? Make this a part of your expectation and responsibility. If you struggle with giving, then maybe this is not the time to seek an apostolic mentor. The story of the widow with the two mites in **Luke 21:1-4** is one of the most beautiful love stories about giving I've ever read.

Her giving reflected her *heart condition* toward God.

The Apostle Paul was so frustrated with the lack of financial support among the congregation that he had to return to work. How phenomenal it would have been if they had helped him!

I keep my face before the Lord concerning Dr. K, as should anyone in a mentoring relationship. It is my prayer to be the best steward and student over this gift I've been given. I look for the Lord to keep my heart submissive, honorable and respectful concerning our relationship – less I wreck it with familiarity and my mentor becomes common to me.

I approached my relationship with my pastor in the same way and God has kept those boundaries. I can remember saying to him, "I am thankful for our friendship, honesty and openness. But I never want to forget the capacity in which God has sent you into my life.

"I need the good shepherd, not a familiar friend. I need the power of God upon your life to help me heal, trust again, believe in myself and believe in the congregation of the Lord."

I've learned that when God sends WORTHY leaders into our lives for a specific work, we must seek Him in honoring the gift. Hold on to this as we move into the next section.

THE PROPHETIC POSTURE OF THE MENTEE

Will you mentor me?

This is one of the main questions people ask me in ministry today. I receive emails, social networking inquiries, etc. from people globally to align and find pasture daily.

It tells me one thing: People really need help!

There are people whom I have mentored that had tremendous potential, and because they postured themselves correctly in our mentoring relationships they SOARED and are continuing to soar. They are truly fruit producers in the Kingdom with tremendous impact, influence, authority and power within their measure.

These, however, are far and few in between.

Others hear the word, and it falls to dry ground – never germinating beyond a temporary high and a couple of completed projects. They live in frustration and lack the humility, discipline and push to move forward. They are beautiful people at heart and are walking with the Lord, but the reality is: Some people will never reach their potential. They are stuck deeply in self.

As a mentor, I've learned to move on. You cannot force a horse who has been led to water to drink. Neither will I pour into a dry well that has an inability to absorb the water, lest it becomes a stagnant, bacteria filled pool and a hindrance to advancing the Kingdom. Mentors must realize that at the end of the day the mentee is FULLY RESPONSIBLE for his or her own growth and development if they are sitting under a mentor who is giving them their very best.

Let me say this a different way. God has given us His absolute best. How we respond to HIS BEST is completely up to us. Period.

MENTORS WILL NOT CHASE YOU

John 7:37 CJB says, *"Now on the last day of the festival, Hoshana Rabbah, Yeshua stood and cried out, **IF ANYONE IS THIRSTY, let him KEEP COMING to me and DRINKING!** Whoever puts his trust in me, as the Scripture says, **rivers of living water will flow from his inmost being!**"*

Christ is basically saying that those who are thirsty will chase after the water to quench their thirst. We see it again in **Revelation 22:17**. They won't stand by waiting for someone to bring it to them.

Mentees need guidance, not the mentor. **While there is mutual learning simply by relationship, there is still only one teacher.** Sure, we can learn from one another and glean... but in a mentoring relationship, the mentor is the principle teacher.

Mentees who really WANT mentorship, will facilitate their learning by any means necessary. I practice making good use of my time with my mentor – notebook and Bible in hand. Is this not the posture of a student and a teacher?

Is this not how God wants us to be when we are learning of Him – focused, attentive? I take extensive notes when I am learning from my mentor and I review them often. Learning for me is not an *appearance* but an active practice.

I don't just stop there. I have asked the Lord to help me make what I learn applicable to my heart and mind. I want to get it!

Mentees must do what it takes to facilitate their OWN learning, progress and success. I firmly believe when a mentee realizes that Christ really LIVES IN THAT SENT MENTOR, they would SEE GOD at work.

In addition, I make it a practice not to mentor people who fail to cultivate their own spiritual life with fierceness and fervency. No mentor should unless they are discipling new believers or walking with struggling ones. Even then, proper boundaries must be established.

I do not pull teeth or try to force people to do anything. I used too, but realized this was Holy Spirit's role not mine. Some people ARE NOT hungry for the things of God.

Have you ever met someone who has been in school for 15 years, but have never earned a single certificate or degree? They are not desperate to finish or graduate. They literally just take a class and accumulate debt. If you ask them about the classes they have wasted thousands of dollars on – they haven't learned a thing! For me, that's what it is like trying to pour into someone who has not fully removed the lid off their jar. All the water is running down the sides of the container onto the table and floor.

This isn't just about their unfinished projects, but it is a pretty good reflection of their lives.

People who are in this place are not properly postured for *apostolic* mentoring. They need an evangelist to motivate them or a pastor to lead them. A different kind of anointing is needed for someone in this place – one that can hold their hands and struggle through the process with them.

So, if a person needs a pastoral mentor *then find* a pastoral mentor. Get what you NEED not what you want!

THE TRANSITIONING MENTEE

Apostolic mentorship is most often for those who are TRANSITIONING from one spiritual plane of discipline, maturity, understanding and responsibility to another more elevated one. These people are not moving from the baby stage to maturity; but from an already mature phase into an even greater one. They are moving from the *contending-Jacob-phase* to *the-promised-Israel*. They are moving from the *Joseph-Potiphar's-wife-phase* to *governor of the city*. **What I want you to see here is that apostolic mentoring is designed to meet mentees in one of the most significant "places of transition" they will ever face in their spiritual lives.**

Mentees who are in this place do not need a cheerleader to survive or thrive. They've crossed that road. They do not need handholding and stroking. They are not struggling with those who do not know who they are or where they are going at all. These mentees just need strong apostolic leadership to help clarify their purpose and/or direction; stabilize them; help them navigate; stand with them; and provide *revelatory* teaching beyond what they have in a specific area or overall to bring them into the deeper waters of the Spirit! For some mentees, new chapters will be written in their book. For others, there will be the closing of an entire book; and the opening of volume two!

Quite honestly, I am in volume two right now, and will never pick up volume one again except as a reminder of God's grace and lessons learned.

Serious mentees, here are some steps you can take to ensure you are postured correctly to receive an INTIMATE apostolic mentor into your life. The items listed below are in no particular order of significance.

A mentee seeking an INTIMATE "apostolic" mentor should:

- **Have a stable, grounded spiritual life.** They should not enter the mentoring relationship looking for discipleship, and in some instances parenting. Not every apostolic mentor has the grace to stand as a spiritual parent in a person's life. Be clear about your expectations, so the mentor can be clear about their capabilities and limitations.

- **Practice the concepts of Biblical honor and respect.** The mentor has their place in the relationship; and mentees have their place in the relationship. It is important not to confuse the two by crossing boundaries. Establish what honor and respect looks like up front through conversation. Know it is a mutual exchange.

- **Be transparent and truthful.** As trust is established, allow your life to be an open book. This includes sharing about your past spiritual journey, previous mentoring relationships, successes, failures, etc. Vulnerability is good in a place of safety and trust.

- **Be open and compassionate toward your mentor.**
  They are people with lives, feelings and expectations
  for their relationship with you. Interact with them
  within the compassion of Christ, just as you would
  have them interact with you. Discuss what this might
  look like to avoid conflict and misunderstandings.

- **Practice humility.** Always maintain a humble
  assessment of your role in the Kingdom and in
  relationship with your mentor. You should never have
  to abdicate your authority in your mentor's presence;
  but neither should there be a posture of haughtiness,
  arrogance or pride. (I REALLY LEARNED THIS
  FROM MY MENTOR!) This will also enable the
  mentee to better receive correction and /or alignment.

- **Develop a heart for the mentor, a Godly love.** Ask
  the Lord to give you the heart of your mentor. This
  simply means you will see them through the eyes of
  the Lord, full of compassion – just as you desire them
  to see you! It means you will be able to consider
  things in light of your mentor's mantle, personality
  make-up and passion for Christ. It will enable you to
  understand the intent of the mentor in his or her
  instructions for you. Make this a prayer.

- **Never compete with your mentor.** Instead,
  recommend your mentor, collaborate with your
  mentor, build with your mentor as in a partnership.
  They are there to help and work with you, not simply
  watch you work. Make life easier for yourself, USE
  THEIR RESOURCES in your own life and especially
  within your own ministry. Make their work, as I do
  with my own mentor, core resources for your ministry
  team. Be a mutual help, not a hindrance!

- **Be an eager student.** Not only should you be eager to learn from your mentor, but the mentee should be a continuous student of the Word of God and the ways of the Lord. Develop necessary spiritual disciplines; and show yourself a ready student by purchasing, reading and listening to ALL your mentor's books, messages, video teachings, etc.

  DO NOT expect handouts. Rather, become an investor. I have a "Dr. K" library in my home. I study her books BEFORE I study others. People should sow into what they VALUE!

  I don't have to "pray" about that because the Lord SENT her to me in an apostolic capacity. I encourage you to use what you draw from your mentor's teachings to ask questions, deepen your understanding and receive what you need from mentorship.

  Many times, what you have been longing for will be in their spiritually inspired products, trainings and courses. Why make the mentor work harder? Learn as much as possible on your own from them.

- **Develop a teachable spirit.** Yes, you may have heard some things before. You may believe you know a little bit more, and could be entirely true! However, posture yourself to listen with fresh ears. Apostolic mentors have a way of breathing new life to the common. Being teachable doesn't simply mean sitting down and listening like a mannerable student; but searching out what you hear for greater understanding.

- **Pursue your mentor.** We've talked about this, but I've added some additional info here. Your mentor should never have to chase you down or wonder where you are under normal circumstances. Recognize that you are the one who needs a mentor, not the other way around.

  Pursuit involves initiating and returning phone calls, emails and texts in a timely manner; attending all functions that become available as you can; serving that mentor in a Godly capacity at every opportunity; or otherwise posturing yourself to receive.

  Under normal circumstances, mentors do not CHASE mentees. Ever. The mentee has the primary responsibility of initiating interactions with the mentor. I've lost quite a few people here because they selfishly think it is my responsibility to chase them down. Nope. Not happening.

- **Practice following through.** Don't be a ball dropper. This is a sign of immaturity and a lack of commitment. Whatever assignments you are given or training you agree to, see it through to the end. Failing in this area is a clear sign the mentee is not ready for apostolic mentoring.

- **Initiate conversations and questions.** You are supposed to lead in the process of drawing wisdom, revelation and solutions from your mentor. Not the other way around. Constantly position yourself to let the mentor know what you need. Don't assume the mentor will know "by the Spirit." This is a ridiculous assumption – especially if they are mentoring other people, traveling, working, have family, etc. Be realistic in this.

- **Involve your mentor in your activities, projects and events.** Whether they accept or not, extend the invitation to be a part. This includes getting input and insight in your planning processes as well as feedback or even participation.

- **Be open about your weaknesses and strengths.** Mentors are often looking for ways to strengthen and serve you. Be open to discussing these areas and obtaining counsel.

- **Be open to accountability.** Apostolic mentors provide accountability. The purpose of accountability is to assist the mentee with upholding their responsibilities in the Gospel – in their character, integrity and ministry. Mentees should find a "safe place" in their Godly mentors. This, as I see it, isn't about covering someone – but standing with them in their efforts to honor the vocation of the Gospel.

In ministry, I've experienced some difficult struggles in marriage, family, ministry relationships, and even some deeply personal things. I believe one of the primary reasons why we see so many ministers fall into sin, commit suicide or fall under the pressure of ministry and quit is because they didn't have accountability and support. Who can they turn to for needed counsel, restoration, defense, etc.

Yes, our best friends can help, but some situations are beyond the counsel, AUTHORITY and spiritual capabilities of our buddies. Some INTIMATE apostolic mentors can navigate these kinds of situations well.

- **Make sure your mentoring expectations are well-rounded and realistic.** As a mentor, I have found this to be a major issue. Realize upfront that while your mentors are apostolic and prophetic, they are not slaves, mind readers, police, gods, idols or any of those things from an unhealthy fantasy world.

  Mentors cannot be everywhere and do everything. And you are probably not the only person whom they mentor. Healthy, Christ-centered expectations should reflect this. Mentors do not have to do what "the mentees" want. Rather, they are positioned to do what is needed and what is best regardless of any prophetic dreams, visions or prophesies a person believes they have had.

  Just because a mentee may be famous or well-known, it doesn't warrant any special treatment, favors or liberties.

- **Be faithful and consistent givers or financers of the INTIMATE mentor's ministry.** This is self-explanatory. This concept of giving, as I see it, goes beyond the action of giving offerings and alms.

  There should be a passion and desire to sow beyond the ordinary in the good ground where you are reaping or will reap a *tremendous, life altering* harvest. Do not commit spiritual robbery in mentorship. There is no TRUE HARVEST in anything that lacks a seed that costs you **(2 Sam. 24:24)**. It's not necessarily about the amount. If you only have a little, give what you can give. If you can give beyond that make every effort to do so.

- **Be trustworthy, confidential and loyal.** These terms, for the most part, are also self-explanatory. Mentees should be people who PRACTICE trust and confidentiality within this relationship. Just as the mentee expects this from the mentor, so does the mentor expect this from the mentee. Don't emulate the heart of Judas or Haman concerning your mentor.

- **Practice accountability.** Accountability enables a mentee to share the burden of life and ministry. The apostolic mentor is often able to place situations in perspective, provide counsel, develop strategies or create effective solutions.

  Accountability is critical to maintaining one's authority and good name in the faith, and can cover numerous areas. Decide if this is something you will need from your mentor.

- **Be responsive to the directives of the mentor.** Apostolic mentorship is dependent upon activation. Be participatory in all aspects of the process. The mentee must be postured to take military orders and work through the process of walking them out.

- **Expect covenant relationship.** In intimate mentorship, covenant relationship should be the goal. There is an anointing, defense and protection in covenant for the mentee and the mentor.

- **Be a defender and protector of your mentor and your relationship.** Don't worry. This isn't a twisted or scary request. Just as you stand for truth and understanding in relationships with family, close friends and loved ones, you should take a posture of standing for truth with your mentor as well - defending and protecting the relationship. This stand is part of covenant.

In my life, I do not entertain conversations, gossip or challenges that would wound my mentor, undermine or damage our relationship. Recently, I traveled with Dr. K and three additional women she mentored on a road trip.

There was one woman within the group who began to mistreat Dr. K and another woman with us. Efforts by Dr. K to confront this behavior or bring reconciliation only escalated the disrespect this woman exhibited. She didn't want peace. She didn't want to work it out. She simply wanted to ride in the car, abuse Dr. K and another woman who was with us on the trip.

It was appalling. In all my days in ministry, I had never seen anything like that.

It's like this woman was determined to make all of us miserable by having a literal temper tantrum – *literally like a child* – in the car. My only recourse was to rise up in righteous indignation, take charge and ensure that things did not escalate further. It was ugly! This person refused reason. And because I witnessed the entire situation, I could speak directly into it.

Please understand I am not speaking of any kind of strange and weird defense of Dr. K. Rather, I am speaking of standing against blatant disrespect and disregard for everyone else in the vehicle as well. I have done this for people in the grocery store or in restaurants because it was RIGHT in the eyes of the Lord. If I would do it for a stranger, how much more is required for those we entrust with growing or building us in the Lord?

Paul would have never confronted the Corinthian church so severely or defended his apostleship if the people within the congregation he oversaw had stood against those bringing division and destruction. This was my stand. I made a point to ensure that this woman was never alone with Dr. K for the duration of the trip.

It was only when this woman got into her own vehicle and drove away that I could stand down. You may never encounter a situation like this. But, if it occurs would you be willing to defend your mentor? If something went awry that could have escalated into a dangerous situation would you be a God-centered witness?

Remember, this is also reciprocal.

- **Be a reconciler.** Be prepared to confront perceived or actual offense in love; and be quick to forgive. A mentor or mentee should never be okay with leaving misunderstandings or disagreements unanswered. Despite past hurt and fears, work overtime to create an environment of trust that leads to reconciliation and/or restoration.

- **Be an intercessor.** The mentee should posture themselves as an active intercessor for their mentor.

- **Be an exhorter.** A mentee should have the heart of an exhorter concerning the mentor, one that is fortified in strengthening the mentor in the faith.

- **Be ordained by your apostolic mentor.** Seal your alignment with your apostolic mentor through ordination. I have been ordained multiple times over the course of my life within the local congregation. I have held roles from deacon to prophet. However, when I aligned with Dr. K, I was given specific instructions to remove those ordinations, and walk only under this new one.

I believe this is significant because it CLOSES the chapter on old seasons. It removes the handprints of the past. For me, there was a literal stripping away of the old and a complete walking into the new. It is always best to make a clear alignment. In addition, I sensed a portal open over my life that literally snatched me into a new realm of thinking, seeing and operating in the gifts of the Spirit.

If ever anyone could experience what may have happened to the 70 in Numbers 11 after they were commissioned by God, I believe I experienced it that day.

To this day, I have never had an experience that comes close to this. I was also healed of a brain mass that night. I know my healing, in this instance, came by way of alignment.

- **Don't rush the mentoring process.** I'm going to explain this a bit. Sometimes, mentees can have deadlines concerning when they are supposed to have accomplished something or when they believe they should have received breakthrough. God does not work on "perceived" schedules. It's quite possible you could have missed Him with that time line. Holy Spirit should have freedom in mentoring relationships! Not demands. **Effective MENTORS won't miss it!**

- **Travel with your mentor for ministry.** One of the greatest privileges I have had is traveling with Dr. K. She likes to drive, so this makes our trips quite amazing! I have miracle testimonies about our time together on the road. Plus, she has a great sense of humor, is fun and easy going. *No one* could plan the things that happened to us in the Spirit... seriously! In her own words, she has described some of those encounters as: "Just incredible!"

  Well, I highly recommend traveling with your mentor if possible. These are rare opportunities to observe the apostolic grace on your mentor's life, and learn to navigate apostolically in these environments. What I enjoy most is our time after the meetings in which we discuss the message, and sometimes ways to enhance delivery and presentation. It blesses me to see how open Dr. K is to feedback, and suggestions on how to connect with people.

- **Seek to replicate your mentor's revelation.** This does not mean clone or twin them. Be fully YOURSELF! However, it is the hope of every mentor that their mentees or students will replicate what is in them. My spirit is so open to what the Lord has for me in my mentor's life.

As a result, I retain a massive amount of what I hear the first time and apply it. Anything I do not understand eventually becomes tremendous revelation to me! I don't reject what she teaches when I don't agree, I let it marinate in my Spirit.

Eventually, I will run into that moment of clarity in which it makes sense and changes my perspective. It is important to me that I teach those I mentor what I am learning from her also, to help them cross into higher. Isn't this the beauty of mentorship?

- **The people you watch and listen to on television and on your device, can only be passive mentors.** Mentees know them ONLY through their audio, books or teachings and maybe viewing them within crowds at a few conferences.

They have zero access to their character and lives outside of what is public. You may admire them, but they will never stand with you like an active APOSTOLIC mentor.

If this is the case, why would the mentee place more weight on what they are learning from a passive mentor than they are from an INTIMATE one. Much can be gleaned from passive mentoring; but how much more can be received when the mentee OPENS himself up to receive from the INTIMATE mentor he or she "chose" who was indeed sent by God.

One of the most disturbing practices I've seen among the Body are people who follow and give to complete strangers over their own pastors, apostles and leaders. They will beg, borrow and steal to go to conference 2,000 miles away, buy all of this product—and won't invest in those who labor with them.

This is abuse! It is an affront to God! And sometimes, it's also clouded deeply in religion. If this has been something common to your life, I strongly advise you to ask yourself these hard questions: Why do I value the advice of others OVER the advice of my intimate mentor? Why do I believe the anointing in these people or places is greater than what is before me? Am I really willing to follow my mentor with a greater fervency than I follow these passive mentors?

My intent is not to give you a check list, but to provide you with insight into how a "mentee" can be effectively postured to maximize their relationship with an apostolic mentor. On the same note, this isn't one sided. The mentor has responsibilities as well.

God takes mentoring seriously.

In looking at these areas of preparation, I hope you are gaining greater insight into "what you want" and "what you expect" from a mentoring relationship. I cannot reiterate how important it is to layout those expectations clearly to avoid conflict and confusion while at the same time being open to the Lord having His way in those relationships.

Apostolic mentoring, believe it or not, is one of the greatest demonstrations of COVENANT LOVE we can experience in the Body of Christ outside of the love of Christ, the sacred bond of marriage and family.

In addition, INTIMATE mentoring should be as much HEALING AND RESTORATIVE as it is apostolic. After all, the apostolic exists – in part - to save and restore.

John 13:23 NKJV, *"Now there was leaning on Christ's bosom one of IIis disciples, **whom Christ loved.**"*

John 18:10-11 NIV, *"Then Simon Peter, who had a sword, drew it and struck the high priest's servant, cutting off his right ear. (The servant's name was Malchus.)* **Jesus commanded Peter,** *Put your sword away! Shall I not drink the cup the Father has given me?"*

The next day John was there again with two of his disciples. When he saw Jesus passing by, he said, "Look, the Lamb of God! When the two disciples heard him say this, they followed Jesus. ~ John 1:3537

IDENTIFYING YOUR GOD ORDAINED MENTOR

We have covered significant ground. We are going to build out here and provide tools to help identify your God ordained mentor.

There was a time when I was easily impressed by popular ministers who could prophesy well, run mega ministries and who lived in outward prosperity. I was mesmerized by the entourages, and the networks of spiritual sons and daughters. I longed to be in the inner circle, believing I could access some super-special anointing there that was better than what everyone else had. And if a person preached well, caused people to hit the floor as they prayed, could wave their hand and knock people out, and get crowds of thousands riled up, I thought I was witnessing the power of God.

I had a full-blown movie-star mentality about ministers and ministries. I wanted to be like those people. And for a long time, I saw them as better than myself. Some of you may be able to identify with these truths from my life. My own idolatry ensnared me **(James 1:14-15).**

God's word is so true.

The scales on my eyes concerning who I was and where I was in that season was stripped away. After working in leadership up close in both small Christian communities and mega ministry environments, I literally became sick at what I saw at the hands of preachers, their entourages, spiritual sons and daughters, and even families. What was scarier was when I began looking at my own ministry. I was mimicking their man-made patterns and following their corrupt leadership styles.

There I was, creating the same type of environments that bred idolatry, super-star mindsets and sought selfish gain. Every day I am grateful the Lord snatched me out of this before it took root in my heart. Some of my brothers in the Lord are still caught up in all the crazy today. My heart breaks for them.

I saw leaders do everything from manipulate the pocket books of unsuspecting people; cause people to uproot their lives from different states or countries; and position themselves as god over people's lives – controlling everything from their emotions and living arrangements to their very calling and purpose. I watched some become homeless at the hands of these people they so faithfully served. It was sickening.

The abuse can be vicious. It is devastating to know so many are destroyed by people perpetrating "doing God's work." There are charlatans in the temple! The last straw for me came at a major prayer conference when I had dropped everything to serve for seven days with this well-known minister. I was a paid staff member at the time, but rarely got compensated fairly for my service. *(This was years ago, long before I met Dr. K!)*

When we arrived, our accommodations were crammed and we literally had to beg for food while being worked like slaves. I am not lying to you! We were working around the clock, and no one brought food to us – the staff or volunteers. I can remember delivering something to the green room, and being treated so badly by those inside, including that minister. They were living like kings while the people making it happen were suffering. But because so many had stars in their eyes, they counted their suffering as godly. It was "faith service" for them and they really believed a blessing was in it for their lives.

People of God, I'm not exaggerating. In fact, I wish I was exaggerating.

This really happened. I had someone say this to me during this "prayer" conference: "This is why we are to work as if it is unto the Lord." I will just leave that statement right there.

I quit working for this ministry the minute I stepped foot in Atlanta. Let's just say my eyes were fully opened… and I experienced one of the greatest purgings I've endured in my walk with Christ. All of that idolatry came down, and every ungodly lust I had that led me there was gone.

From my experiences, and I've had some way worse than this, I learned some difficult lessons. I wrote this book so you won't have to go through similar painful experiences to learn these lessons! Among the greatest lesson I learned was this: "Loving God means honoring people." This became one of the lenses by which I recognize God's heart in operation. I stopped following ministries on television and popular personalities after this. I stopped putting financial seeds into these ministries and started sowing locally. I can't vouch for other people, but I know what I did and how I used to be before I transitioned to a new perspective and way of pure ministry. But I also know what I have learned from these experiences.

I spent most of my natural life being mistreated at the hands of those who should have loved and cared for me. Now, there I was letting other people abuse me under the guise of religion. If God was for me - and I began questioning that during this time - then He alone would help me connect with people who would not pimp, prostitute or rape my heart. He would connect me with those who were for me.

So, I walked away from everything – all the abuses and mistreatment, double standards, shattering betrayals and lies. God dealt with the role my idolatry bound heart played in this too. **I was looking for people to meet my spiritual needs, not God. I was looking for popularity and fame, not God. I was looking for parents not mentors, and in doing so I compromised myself tremendously.**

I walked away from the local church and nearly all ministry friendships and alliances (networks, associations, women's groups, mentoring relationships, etc.). I left my family and God altogether.

By the time I met Dr. K, I was in the best place I had been in years. There was no way I could have met her sooner, because I was not ready. With all of this behind me, I had walked into my calling and was operating in a clear heart and mind – ready for the next place.

CONFRONTING SPIRITUAL ABUSE

Godly mentors do not practice spiritual abuse! Period.

Spiritual abuse is defined as ANY type of abuse committed against a person who is standing in the supposed safety, confidentiality and counsel of a person with spiritual authority over them. The abuse occurs when the authority figure uses abusive methods to manipulate or control his or her members, mentees or congregants with scripture, spiritual influence or spiritual authority.

Spiritual abuse can happen to people of all ages and in diverse kinds of ministry settings. Even the most elect can find themselves in spiritually abusive situations. No person ANYWHERE is immune.

My insight here is not an attempt to cover this topic in significant detail. I am simply bringing some key issues to light, and urging mentees to recognize them. I also want our discussion here to (1) affirm that spiritual abuse is real and relevant; (2) that mentees have the right and duty to reject spiritual abuse; (3) God is NOT PLEASED with abusive leadership, nor does He ordain this type of behavior; (4) God does not place people in abusive situations to test them; (5) mentees have the right to say no to abuse, refuse to participate in abuse or be a part of abusive situations and coverups; and (6) mentees can walk away from abusive leaders and situations without explanation.

I am not an expert or licensed counselor, but I have fallen prey to spiritual abuse. Much of my insight here comes from that place; as well as walking with or counseling people who have or are healing from horrific violations by people in ministry. In many instances, passages like **Hebrews 13:17** have propelled false teachings to justify it.

The scripture reads: *"Have confidence in your leaders and* ***submit to their authority, because they keep watch over you*** *as those who must give an account.* ***Do this so that their*** ***work will be a joy, not a burden, for that would be of no*** ***benefit to you.***"

This passage, just so you know, is a plea for the those in a local body to trust THE GOD in those who are leading them in the faith who have *their best interest* at heart. It is a cry to SUPPORT them in the work of the community by every man doing his part without quarreling and division. It is about serving within the community and supporting the leaders as if you are doing it unto the Lord.

It is about mutually carrying the vision with the pastor or leader as a helper – one to another, and ensuring the members do not become a part of the problem. It has nothing to do with men "OBEYING" men in the ridiculous whims that fly their way. It is not about being a slave.

There is no such thing as *unquestioned* authority among men!

In mentoring relationships, we follow a universal code of honor according to the scriptures: mentor-mentee, teacher-student, father/mother-child, etc. We RESPECT authority and respond appropriately to authority. This, however, DOES NOT MEAN servitude. **Honor is always reciprocal! Respect is always reciprocal!**

As I see it, spiritual abuse is similar to "domestic violence." Instead of one's personal home, it happens within their ministry home or ministry environment, and its victims, often endure it because they love the perpetrator, believe their lies, fear the perpetrator or otherwise find themselves brainwashed, obligated or guilted into accepting it.

They believe they DESERVE to be treated that way. While this issue is discussed more today than in previous decades, it is still not addressed at the level it should be. I've heard stories of people ironing underwear, running bathwater and testing the bubbles in the water of mentors. Ridiculous!

Show me in the New Covenant where Christ or his apostles instituted these practices? This is where our journey begins in looking at healthy relationships. (I am not saying people don't need help in ministry. Do not misunderstand. But some things cross the line. In my life, I served leaders in ministry in ways I wasn't serving my own husband at home. THAT was a problem.)

There is ministry help – which we all need on various levels, and then there is abuse. Check out these common areas of spiritual abuse.

Sexual advances and coercion are NEVER okay in a mentoring relationship.

A mentor does not have permission to rub up against you, playfully massage your thighs or arms, or to engage in any unwanted, inappropriate touching. They do not have the right to share pornography with you, even as a joke or ask you what you think about it.

They should not complement your body parts; torment you with dirty jokes; or suggest you are sexually frustrated. The mentor should not discuss their sexual frustrations or prowess in their singleness or in their marriage; bore holes through you with lustful gazes; or proposition you for oral sex or intercourse.

Your mentor should never sexually assault you and expect it to be overlooked with an apology. Your mentor should never coerce or bully you into sex, or to call you a tease or temptress. Appropriate language should be used in all conversations.

A *leader* I once trusted said to me once, "I am sorry for what I did. But if you tell anyone I will deny it. No one will believe you anyway. I've been a preacher for a long time."

The devastation from sexual assault, molestation or rape is indescribable whether you were assaulted with words, devoured inappropriately with a person's eyes or physically accosted. I do not believe this type of behavior is the norm, but it does happen to MEN AND WOMEN (also children and young adults) far more often than we realize!

If this is happening or has happened to you (past or present), know it is not your fault. Get to a safe place immediately. Get medical help if needed, contact a person you absolutely trust (preferably outside of that environment) for support, and contact the authorities.

This type of behavior is **NEVER** a misunderstanding or mistake! It is always intentional. YOU DO NOT HAVE TO PROTECT YOUR ABUSER! You do not have to carry the shame and humiliation from this. Trust me, they are already looking out for themselves. Protect yourself.

Bullying is unacceptable.

People in positions of authority in ministry groups and settings can use their leadership role and/or influence to intimidate those they oversee to force someone's will, or otherwise try to get them to do what they want. It is not okay for a mentor or anyone on their staff or ministry team to be allowed to persecute, harass, strong-arm or threaten their mentees.

Bullying can be subtle or direct. Shunning can be a part of bullying as well. Leaders will create clicks and then go out of their way to exclude certain people as punishment. Passive-aggressive behavior is sometimes a sign of bullying.

Humiliation can be used as a strategy for submission.

While it can fall under the category of bullying, I believe it warrants a bullet point of its own. Humiliation is the act of intentionally embarrassing or shaming someone in the hope of stripping them of their self-worth, stature, dignity and human value to make them subservient to the leader.

Being spoken to in a condescending way at every possible opportunity is a common humiliation tactic. I had a pastor who I believe hated to hear the sound of my voice. Whenever I had something to say, the pastor would talk over me. If I managed to finish, the pastor seemed to take pleasure in tearing it down in a nice, nasty way – and always before people. I'm not talking about correction in mentorship – that's different.

Over time, I became silent in their presence – afraid to speak, especially around leaders in ministry. It affected me so greatly that I was fearful of praying or prophesying to any leader or pastor that I considered to be of greater stature than myself. For a long time, I experienced the effects of this around other leaders – even trustworthy ones.

Control and manipulation is unacceptable.

In some situations, mentees are cut-off from having any other spiritual relationships or alliances with other ministers or ministries. Leaders can demand exclusivity. This is CONTROL! Period. They twist scripture in such a way that it benefits self. These leaders position themselves as the only true voice for their group and sometimes the congregation. They are generally dictators and rule from the "my way or the highway" mindset. Other opinions or insight is unwelcomed and discouraged. (Again, there should be loyalty and levels of commitment in mentoring relationships. This section is not about that.)

There was a time when I wanted to help other ministers administratively with my skills. I was told by a leader that my gifts, which I was volunteering, *belonged* in service to them only and that this was where my anointing should be put to work. I would be talked out of helping people.

I have also been a part of ministries where people uprooted their whole lives to come serve, only to be left destitute and abandoned when their service was no longer needed!

This also applied to other areas of service that I rendered at that time. I was told repeatedly that I was in rebellion and being disobedient when I did not follow these rules.

Spiritual violence of any kind is unacceptable.

It is never okay to be submitted to corporate force in a ministry setting like adult spankings; being slapped, being yelled at, things thrown at you, things snatched from you, or doors slammed in your face.

The focus of violence is to cause physical and emotional harm. It is a person punishing you, exerting power over you. While this could also fit under the category of bullying, I thought it was worth bringing to the forefront. No Godly leader would treat anyone this way.

People can become angry occasionally, but they do not lash out in rage and violence - ever. This is NOT about having a bad day or even a bad few days. Violence is spiritual abuse. There's nothing to work out here. Leave.

Present manipulative, erroneous Biblical teachings.

Manipulation by false teachings is common. Some people will use their spiritual positions to purport all kinds of heresy to control people. Teachings on spiritual fathering and coverings have messed up so many people! Pastors and leaders have used this to literally rape people of their resources, time, talent, money and sometimes their lives.

These teachings and their leaders often push topics like discipline among leadership and discipline in the household. They also use obligation and guilt to keep people connected, or bound to them. Remember, there is no such thing as blind obedience to men. These teachings must be filtered and weighed in light of the New Covenant to determine was is faithful and true.

Matthew 7:15 KJV, *"Beware of false prophets, which come to you in sheep's clothing, but inwardly **they are ravening wolves.***"

It is important to me that those who read this book know that God is a healer and a restorer. While it might be difficult to understand this right now, there are apostolic mentors who will stand with you whether through a situation, a season or for a lifetime! I believe this book is the hope for this.

CHARACTERISTICS OF A GOD ORDAINED MENTOR

Below, I've created a list of characteristics to help you identify your "God ordained mentor." This list is based on what I have derived from my healthy mentoring relationship with Dr. K, and the model I seek to create with those I mentor intimately.

Remember, every INTIMATE mentoring relationship is unique. Because of this, I encourage you to use this list as a baseline for defining what characteristics are essential to you in "identifying your God ordained mentor."

It is my perpetual prayer that the list, or should I say tools, rip hirelings from their ungodly foundations. I pray it reveals facades, collapses sandcastles and exposes merchandisers in your life.

I pray that hope for your well-being will spring forth like a fountain at the foundations, so that God's "pure" love and *intent* for you will be made known.

I pray for your continued growth, development, advancement and success until we all come into the unity of the faith. I pray that every apostolic push found in this book and list be a light unto your path and a lamp to your feet.

I pray for your endurance in the waiting season, and for preparation in the now. I declare your wholeness and healing, and for the understanding of the apostolic mind to arise within you. May the apostolic mentoring relationship God has ordained for you reveal itself on the rock directly in the face of our fierce, faithful and loving God.

(This list is in no particular order. Also, we already know the mentor will fiercely love God, His word and operate in His fear. We are simply building upon those foundations.)

YOUR INTIMATE APOSTOLIC MENTOR WILL:

- **Know that they are your mentor.** Eventually, God will show the spiritual mentor that they are assigned to you in some way. Allow the mentor the freedom to determine what that might look like. And remember, relationship must be built and then expanded.

- **Have a heart for you.** Christ had a heart for the disciples He mentored intimately. They were people He genuinely cared about. Mentoring them was not a chore, but a pleasure and delight. Your mentor should not be aggravated by your presence or feel obligated to help you.

- **Never bring you into slavery or idolatry.**

- **Herd the mentee into series of classes, networks or programs that fail to reflect the mentees calling, purpose or spiritual needs.** As an artisan and worshipper, those kinds of programs have little value within those environments.

- **Be transparent and vulnerable.** Apostolic mentors are not hidden in their spirituality. Christ's humanity and spirituality were visible before those he mentored intimately. There is an expectation of truth and vulnerability concerning the mentor's struggles, challenges, burdens, life lessons, etc. The mentee should not be blindsided by the mentor's secrets. (This is mutual.)

- **Will be Kingdom producers.** Apostolic mentors will have tremendous fruit, ministry evidence, experience and power. *They cannot be a novice. Look for their work, not just the talk!*

- **Invest in your potential.** The mentor should see their role in your life as an investment of teaching, training, time and resources. The beauty here is that your mentor WILL SEE the potential, and pour into the mentee accordingly.

- **Become a safe place for confession and accountability**. As relationship develops, mentees should have a place of refuge and safety in bearing burdens. Accountability, healing and HELP rests within the relationship.

- **Listen to you and hear you.** Your apostolic mentor will not be concerned only with his or her viewpoint or perspective. They will not attempt to FORCE your mind or your will.

Rather, there will be a place for mutual discussion, mutual learning, understanding and meeting of the heart and mind. Most importantly, they will take the time to listen, and really invest in trying to understand. It is good to be heard – able to share your heart without rushing or condemnation.

- **Respect what you are passionate about**. Your apostolic mentor WILL NEVER devalue or minimize your interests, ministry calling or vision for ministry. They will offer correction, wisdom, insight, guidance and direction to align you… but give you the freedom to come into your own understanding.

- **Never cause you to be fearful.** Your apostolic mentor should not instill ungodly fear inside of you toward him or her - shutting down your confidence, strength and voice with intimidation and control. I've met powerful pastors and leaders who are completely timid and powerless around their leaders and mentors. It is like they become like small children.

- **Want to forge a strong relationship.** Christ spent time with his disciples. He taught them, but He also hung out with them, ate with them and learned who they were as people. He knew their temperament and passions.

He shared his passion for ministry with them, declared his love for them, and nearly everywhere he traveled he took them with him. Peter, James and John were so close that they would steal away with him. As a result, they witnessed some of the most critical times in his life and ministry.

- **Care about your past, present and future.** Christ was concerned with things that hindered and propelled his mentees. He was quick to confront and overthrow the past, meet them in the present and launch them into their future. He was involved in their lives, and concerned about their condition.

- **Be honest and authentic.** Christ was honest with his disciples, ensuring their they did not live in a place of delusion and fantasy concerning themselves, the world around them, the way of the Kingdom or the Gospel message. He brought strong discipline and alignment to their lives without apology, and lived his life completely open before them. He never hid his tears, vulnerabilities or weaknesses from them.

  They even saw his sorrow, pain and fear in the Garden of Gethsemane. Most of all, they witnessed his rise from it. **Hebrews 5:7** states, *"During the days of Jesus' life on earth, he offered up prayers and petitions with fervent cries and tears to the one who could save him from death, and he was heard because of his reverent submission"*

- **Be accessible and available.** Christ was a present help to his mentees. Never once did He cut himself off to them except for personal prayer. Never once did He abandon any of them, including Judas Iscariot, whom He knew was plotting His demise.

- **Be consistent and stable in their efforts.** Christ was consistent and stable in his behaviors, teachings, responses, attitudes, etc. There was no wishy-washy, strange and weird behavior exemplified among his mentees.

He didn't love them one day, hate them the next. Even when Peter cut the ear off a soldier and abandoned Him, Christ came in correction, counsel and wisdom. Yet, He was never cruel.

- **Not pimp or prostitute the mentee.** This part might anger some people, but here goes. Mentorship will not be on financial demand, like a buy-here pay-here. True apostolic leaders would never use their mentees as cash machines or demand payment for INTIMATE mentorship. Period. Giving should be TAUGHT, regular, expected and encouraged, but the mentee should NEVER be forced, coerced, threatened or bullied into giving.

Mentees should long to give financially to those who feed them spiritually – especially their INTIMATE apostolic mentor. Yet, the mentor should never withdraw his hand or counsel because the mentee does not. Remember, it's the work of the MINISTRY. **To do so is cruel and unusual behavior that is not demonstrated by Christ or his apostles.** Period. Don't fall for crazy Old Covenant teachings that are manipulated to say otherwise.

Men have all kinds of ways of justifying ungodly behavior, but MENTEES NEED TO KNOW that they are clearly looking at the ways of men – not the way of God. Don't fall prey to this kind of prostitution. Search the New Covenant for yourself. **The bottom line is this, many mentors are nothing more than hirelings. Covenant LOVE does not have price tags before the Father, the Son and Holy Spirit.** Paying for classes, workshops, etc. is no different than paying for school or attending a conference. The two should not be confused.

- **Set clear expectations.** You will never have to guess what your mentor wants. There will be no games or manipulation. Mentoring expectations will be made clear. (one word)

- **Be extremely revelatory.** Apostolic mentors should have revelation, counsel and insight that extends beyond your own reservoir. They should be able to pull you into deep waters, be the catalyst for expanding your capacity and providing tools to stretch your faith. The revelatory realm should be WIDE OPEN to them.

- **Enjoy your company.** At no time should you be tolerated in your mentoring relationship.

- **Will stand and defend the mentee.** There is an expectation of defense in mentoring relationships, especially when there is honesty, integrity and truth.

- **The mentor should stand with the mentee during the challenging times as well as the celebratory ones.** Abandonment should not be an option. Christ exemplified this well.

- **Make a way for the mentee.** The mentor will do his or her part in opening doors for help, resources and opportunities.

- **Want to see the mentee soar.** The mentor should never block the power of God inside the mentee. It should be an honor for the mentor to see the mentee thrive and flourish in his or her calling.

- **Give their mentees POWER, not just knowledge and information.** A true mentor will empty his or her arsenal and outfit the mentees with every tool needed for empowerment, prosperity, effectiveness and success during their relationship.

- **Never have the mentee abdicate his or her authority.** The mentor should never force the mentee to relinquish his or her authority in any aspect of their relationship. In fact, the mentor should be concerned with the mentee walking in the fulness of his or her authority. Not only was this demonstrated in my life by my pastors, but more profoundly demonstrated through my apostolic mentor. There should be an expectation for the mentee to always be free to be themselves, not suppressed. In the same way, the mentee should honor the mentor.

- **Should honor the mentees ministry.** At no time should the mentor usurp the authority of the mentee in his or her ministry meetings, conferences or events. There should be a mutual respect and honor between the mentor and the mentee.

  If my apostolic mentor is attending one of my meetings, I always introduce my mentor and at some time during the meeting, offer an opportunity for her to share with the group.

- **Will honor your relationships.** Your mentor should never forge "mentoring" relationships with those you are personally mentoring. Nor should you cross boundaries within the relationships of your mentor.

From a *mentor* perspective, I have had situations in which people whom I was mentoring took it upon themselves to infiltrate every key relationship with ministers and ministries in my life. Even going as far as to tell the minister, "Don't tell Apostle Johnson I've been coming to counsel with you."

Talk about evil, underhanded and inappropriate! Like snakes, people will "crawl through" the most profitable of your relationships and attempt to make profit using your reputation, influence, etc. I've even experienced supposed mentees working overtime to turn some of those ministerial connections against me. In times like these, I'm thankful for true connections, people who won't fall prey to the games of evil men.

From a *mentee* perspective, I had a mentor who was counseling my team "secretly." This person was teaching the opposite of everything that I taught, even holding private meetings with them behind my back.

This person caused them to dishonor me, and follow their leadership. I thought I was being helped, but I was being used and undermined at every turn. These actions resulted in the complete destruction of the ministry entrusted to me. **No HONORABLE mentor or mentee would ever engage in such behavior.**

Dr. K said this to me one day, "I would never dishonor you or your ministry in this way." And I made the same commitment to her. This does not mean you cannot interact with people, share in fellowship, take classes, etc. But it does mean that boundaries must be set and agreed upon. These types of things must be worked out in relationship.

Perhaps the most important aspect to draw from these points is this: **Respect and honor runs both ways.**

1 Peter 5:1-5 CJB, *"Therefore, I urge the congregation leaders among you, as a fellow-leader and witness to the Messiah's sufferings, as well as a sharer in the glory to be revealed: shepherd the flock of God that is in your care, exercising oversight not out of constraint, but willingly, as God wants; and not out of a desire for dishonest gain, but with enthusiasm; also not as machers domineering over those in your care, but as people who become examples to the flock.*

"Then, when the Chief Shepherd appears, you will receive glory as your unfading crown. Likewise, you who are less experienced, submit to leaders. Further, all of you should clothe yourselves in humility toward one another, because God opposes the arrogant, but to the humble He gives grace."

I AM IN TROUBLE

If you find that you are currently in a mentoring situation that is not reflective of God's heart for you, there is a way out. More importantly, you must come out! Your life is too important to suffer under leaders who are not prepared for you. However, there are a few things you need to be acutely aware of in situations like this.

- **Discuss with the mentor what you need.** Sometimes, a lack of communication can be the reason why mentoring relationships go awry. Work it out, re-evaluate your expectations to determine your next steps. This is always the preferred step.

- **End the mentoring relationship.** If your current mentoring relationship does not meet the needs that are most critical to you, end it. Pursue a beautiful friendship that does not have a mentoring component if possible. Be sure to have this conversation in a respectful, loving way... that honors the mentor. You do have a choice to pursue other avenues.

- **Often, people mentor from what they have learned.** It is possible that your mentor has a heart for you, but is rooted in tradition, religion and other hindrances that prevent that heart from shining. People grow. I am probably an apt poster child for this topic. Endure the growth process with them through honest conversation and relationship building; or decide to leave. Make an effort to remain friends or at least respectful, appreciative and cordial.

- **You can leave, and I mean instantly.** If abuse is present, LEAVE! This is not optional. It is ridiculous to think you can work through "mistreatment" in this type of relationship. Let the Lord turn your affection toward Him fully. Just like in a domestic violence situation, you can walk out with the clothes on your back and get help. It boils down to one thing: How desperate are you to be free? The journey won't be easy, but it will be worth it. Break the soul tie and choose life!

And a voice from heaven said, this is my Son, whom I love; with Him I am well pleased. ~ Matthew 3:17

BEGOTTEN IN THE GOSPEL

1 Corinthians 4:15 NIV says, *"For though you might have ten thousand instructors in Christ, yet you do not have many fathers; for in Christ Jesus **I have begotten you through the gospel.**"*

The Gospel is not just the message of salvation through the life, crucifixion, death, burial and raising up of the Son of God. It is not about trying to do everything right and accessing a faraway place.

What makes the Gospel special is comprehending that it is a cry to exist fully *within the heart* of a perfect God, who is a perfect Father. It is knowing that he literally moved heaven and earth to provide a way for us to touch his heart and know that great love. It is about sonship, the raising up of Sons of God.

It is never about God raising up sons FOR MEN, but for men continuing to make MAKE DISCIPLES who become the SONS OF GOD. We must grasp this.

The Gospel teaches us about the height, depth and width of His *relentless* covenant love for humanity. In turn, He teaches us how to reproduce that *covenant-love* in and through our own lives at various levels. Apostolic mentoring is one of the dimensions of this reproduction.

For those who recognize, and grab hold of the beauty of apostolic mentoring, it will be transformational to their lives. If you really want this kind of relationship in your life, "I pray right now that you will RECOGNIZE your INTIMATE apostolic mentor when He or she comes."

Many times, people have this visual of what that person might look like or be like. I know I did.

The thing is, my mentor wasn't wrapped up like anyone I had imagined. This isn't a negative statement. It only indicates that I could have missed her because I was looking for what was familiar to me. But I thank God DAILY that I heard Him. Your mentor probably won't look like what you think he or she should either! Don't miss what God has for you because you believe it is going to come a certain way or look a specific way. Be open!

I received a Word through the internet for goodness sake – a Google search to be exact! That has NEVER happened to me. It even shocks me sometimes that I paid any attention to it. But the pressure from the Spirit was so strong that it wouldn't let me go! It came in such a unique way that I couldn't possibly deny that it was the Lord.

Let God meet you in the supernatural!

Sometimes, I close my eyes and picture God calling Abraham friend in my holy imagination. I wonder what it must have been like for the woman with the alabaster box to know that Christ wanted the message of the Gospel to be told synonymously in her memory. And I wonder, what it would have been like for John to lay his head on the physical bosom of Christ.

Their stories testify to more than rules and regulations.

They testify to more than emotions and close friends.

They testify to pure covenant relationship – the kind that begs to be released beyond the business of ministry and the me-doms of men. The message of the Gospel is not multiplied by human hands, but by the operation of covenant love through covenant sons. It's the supernatural at work. It's the supernatural that is being multiplied.

God is CONTINUOUSLY reproducing himself in us. That's what spiritual growth is all about. Paul was literally affirming to Timothy in **1 Corinthians 4:15**, that he was reproducing himself – meaning the Christ in Him through ALIGNMENT.

True apostolic mentors are not interested in collecting people and using you to build a personal empire. Rather, they are interested in *multiplying sons* who are sold out for Christ and whose trajectory is tied to theirs. Remember, alignment is about perfect order or divine order. Things fit where they are supposed to fit!

Our earth is aligned with the sun. If it suddenly stopped its orbit, all planet life would die in a matter of days. Then the earth itself would eventually be consumed by the sun. In God's creation, alignment is life giving to all in its path or influenced by its path.

Being "begotten" or being "reproduced" creates additional paths for alignment that are all connected to the source.

Paul was not taking ownership of Timothy in this passage or claiming any special privilege. Rather, he could see the message God had given him replicated in Timothy's life and ministry. Christ released a similar message over his "begotten" sons – the disciples.

INTIMATE apostolic mentors are committed to the Godly sonship process.

EMBRACE HIS HEALING POWER

Many of us have been hurt by men who, for whatever reason, were not ready to be mentors. Also, many of those reading this have also been the cause of someone's legitimate pain.

Whatever the case, the truth remains that Christ is a forgiver of sin for those who repent with their heart; and He is a healer. This book is evidence of my wholeness from the past. It stands as a witness to my life up to this point before God and His angels.

If I could find wholeness from the level of abuse that I have endured at the hands of men, I am confident that you can also.

Despite the goats and the wolves in sheep's clothing, I have met apostles, prophets, evangelists, pastors, teachers, bishops, elders, etc. who truly love God and His people. They live lives of integrity, and genuinely want to see the Body of Christ understand covenant love.

Are all mentors perfect? Again, no... and neither are the mentees. Yet, we serve a God who is... and who stands as their very present help.

Strong, apostolic mentors may be among a remnant, but they do exist in glory and in power before the Lord. I believe the Lord wants to restore that hope in some of those reading this book right now. He wants to bring you into wholeness from the abuses you've suffered at the hands of men who, quite honestly, were not ready to lead God's people because they didn't have his heart.

Through a renewed heart, I have learned that:

- There are believers who will never harm another person intentionally.

- There are believers who will go to the ends of the earth to provide help without conditions, expectations or selfish gain.

- There are believers who will lay down their lives for friends.

- There are believers who will HELP when thousands have withdrawn their hand.

- There are believers who want to see you excel in your growth, development and success in the Lord.

- There are believers who want to work with you, partner with you and enjoy the Kingdom with you.

Finding this in a mentoring relationship is possible!

I pray that you are fully able to acknowledge, release and forgive those past hurts now, in the name of Jesus. I pray that the spirit of fear concerning leadership and mentorship is broken, and that you have the courage to step out on faith and trust again.

I pray the Lord enhances your spiritual discernment in this hour, identifying who is safe and who is not; who is for you and who is not. I pray that it is made plain and clear. I pray for your courage in breaking away from toxic relationships, communities and organizations; and that every ungodly soul—tie, obligation or hold to them are broken.

I pray that your heart and mind are open for purging, and that you are able to release any and all forms of prostitution, false doctrines, man-made theologies, as well as all forms of religion and tradition that call people into slavery instead of freedom. I pray for your decision making! I declare that you will make supernatural choices and decisions that represent God's heart for your life and not the heart of men.

I pray that you are prepared for your apostolic mentor, and that your mentor is prepared for you. I pray that your expectations represent God's heart for you and your mentor. I pray that in its perfect timing, you will recognize, identify and connect with the apostolic mentor God has for you, in Jesus Name.

Bibliography

Pellicano, Maria. "The Art of Powerful Communication: Aligning your mindset, mission and voice," (Pellicano Creative Consulting: 2016), Victoria Melbourne.

Stanley, Paul D. and J. Robert Clinton, "Connecting: The Mentoring Relationships You Need to Succeed in Life," (Colorado Springs: NavPress, 1992).

ABOUT THE AUTHOR

Theresa Harvard Johnson is best known for her revelatory insight, understanding and apostolic teachings surrounding the ministry of the prophetic scribe and prophetic writing. She has published, contributed to or co-authored more than 19 books including her signature publication, "The Scribal Anointing: Scribes Instructed in the Kingdom of Heaven," which has been taught world-wide. Theresa has a heart for ministry integrity and immersion in the Gospel. She also holds a Master of Divinity in Biblical Studies from Liberty University.

Available Books:
- *Apostolic Mentorship: Critical Tools to Help Creative Artisans Identify their God Ordained Mentor*
- *Identifying & Releasing Chaotic People*
- *Writing & the Prophetic*
- *The Scribal Realm of Dreams & Visions*
- *The Scribal Realm Companion (Dream & Impact Journal)*
- *The Scribal Anointing: Scribes Instructed in the Kingdom of Heaven*
- *The Scribal Companion Student Workbook*
- *Scribal Purpose: 10 Reasons Why God Has Called You to Write*
- *Spiritual Critiquing Literary Works*
- *Literary Evangelism Beyond the Open Mic*
- *The Sin of Spiritual Plagiarism: Unauthorized Vessels*
- *40 Signs of a Prophetic Scribe*
- *Signs of a Scribal Prophet*
- *50 Indisputable Biblical Facts About the Ministry of the Prophetic Scribe*

Email: theresahj@schoolofthescribe.com
Blog: chamberofthescribe.com
School: schoolofthescribe.com

Made in the USA
Columbia, SC
21 September 2021

45201449R00081